THE DUMPSTER FIRE ELECTION

Realistic Dystopian Expectations for the 2020 Presidential Election

JASON SCHENKER

THE DUMPSTER FIRE ELECTION

Realistic Dystopian Expectations for the 2020 Presidential Election

BY JASON SCHENKER

ISBN: 978-1-946197-31-3 *Paperback*
　　　　978-1-946197-32-0 *Ebook*

For the dwindling ranks of
American centrists
in both parties.

CONTENTS

CONTENTS

WRITING ABOUT ELECTIONS

Many people talk about elections and their potential impacts, but they seldom discuss some of the historical numbers around them. And it is rarer still to find a sober, dispassionate discussion of U.S. elections. Unfortunately, I expect this will be an increasingly big problem. It's a key reason why this book's title and content present a dystopian outlook for the 2020 presidential election.

In many ways, *The Dumpster Fire Election* is the third book in my election series. The previous two books were *Midterm Economics* (2018) and *Electing Recession* (2016). In all three of these works, I have tried to present the election outcome drivers in a factual and nonpartisan way. I have also tried to use real data to help shape forecasts for what comes after the election.

As in my previous two election books, the main goal of *The Dumpster Fire Election* is to explore some of the historical political, economic, and financial market data that allow for a contextualization and objective analysis of the imminent U.S. presidential election in a nonpartisan, data-driven way.

This goal of examining data in an original way is to create original research and to contribute to an informed debate about the importance of elections and what the outcomes of the 2018 U.S. midterm elections may hold for financial markets and the economy.

In writing this book, I also considered it extremely important to explore what political, economic, and financial market factors would likely impact the outcome of the presidential election in 2020. Because elections do not happen in a bubble. The world around them matters greatly.

In *The Dumpster Fire Election*, I revisit some of the analysis that was critical in *Electing Recession*. This means that there are a number of topics that you will see again in this book that have changed significantly since 2016, including the current state of the economy and financial markets. Much has changed for financial markets and the economy in the three years since *Electing Recession* was published — and a lot has changed even in the year since *Midterm Economics* was released. But the structure of the analysis and source of much of the data are the same.

But there are also some new topics in *The Dumpster Fire Election* that were not even on our radar in 2016. The risk of election interference on a massive scale by foreign entities using social media as well as the radicalization of identity politics to foster subnational identities that could fracture nationalist identity have become cornerstones of risk going into the 2020 election season. And these risks are the gasoline of the dumpster fire.

Acknowledgements

In addition to wanting to include some new topics and expand on existing ones that I covered in *Electing Recession* and *Midterm Economics*, I want to thank the individuals who have provided support and feedback on this project, including **Nawfal Patel** and my other colleagues at Prestige Economics, as well as everyone at Prestige Professional Publishing who helped me bring this book to fruition.

Finally, and most importantly, I want to thank my family for supporting me as I worked on this book. I dedicated previous books to my loving wife, **Ashley Schenker**, and to my supportive parents, **Jeffrey and Janet Schenker**. Although I have dedicated this book *"For the dwindling ranks of American centrists in both parties,"* it is my family that has supported me in countless ways over the years by providing emotional support and editorial feedback — and by being there for me.

Every time I write a book, it's a crazy experience that spills over into my family life, so to them and to everyone else who helped me in this process: thank you!

And of course, thank you for buying this book. I hope you enjoy *The Dumpster Fire Election*!

~ Jason Schenker

THIS PRESIDENTIAL ELECTION WILL BE A DUMPSTER FIRE

When I was looking for a title to this book, I wanted one that conveyed the risks of political polarization, the potential for inflammatory social media interactions, the potential for interference, and the overall distaste that most Americans are likely to experience the upcoming 2020 presidential election.

There are plenty of titles that could have been suitable. But I also needed a title that I could say on live television. So I passed on titles like *The Shit-show Election* in favor of the more polite — and more zeitgeisty — title *The Dumpster Fire Election*.

In *Midterm Economics*, I wrote about how the outcome of the presidential election of 2016 was a shock to many, but it should not have been. But it was, in fact, a completely foreseeable outcome.

I even noted the potential for a Trump victory in *Electing Recession* back in 2016, noting that the biggest thing Trump had going for him was that presidential elections have become increasingly like reality television.

This is why I was not surprised by Donald Trump's success in clinching the Republican presidential nomination. After all, more Americans voted for *American Idol* in 2012 than in the U.S. presidential election[1] — and Trump was a reality TV star!

While the politics and policies of the Trump administration have shocked and awed, depending on your political perspectives, the next presidential election will soon be upon us, and there are many new questions to consider about the economy, financial markets, and politics.

And we also need to consider the impact and outcome of the 2018 U.S. midterm elections, which were one of the biggest routs in U.S. history for a prevailing party during such a strong economic boom.

And let me make one thing clear at this point: the U.S. economy is in a very strong position, even though there are significant global risks.

As of the publication of this book, the most recent U.S. data, which were for May 2019, reflect a tight job market with a 3.6 percent unemployment rate, which is the lowest unemployment rate since late 1969. Wages were also up 3.1 percent year on year in May. And although GDP growth is likely to slow as U.S. business investment feels the aftereffects of Fed rate hikes in 2018 and a reduction of the Fed's balance sheet, it was at a solid 3.1 percent in Q1 2019.

So the economic situation looks pretty good — for now.

As in my past books on elections, this book will also address political, financial, and economic topics.

Questions Need Answers

In this book, I will attempt to answer some of the most important questions that we should be looking at, including the following:

- **What can the outcome of and the political conditions after the 2018 U.S. midterm elections tell us about the issues and voting that will be most important for the 2020 U.S. presidential election?**

- **Where are the economy and financial markets now, and can the 2020 presidential election impact their outlook?**

- **Trade policy has been a critical cornerstone of the Trump administration's policy actions. What role could trade play in the 2020 presidential election?**

- **What is the relationship between elections and the start of recessions?**

- **What aspects of the political and economic outlook will remain unchanged regardless of the 2020 presidential election outcome?**

- **Are there data that offer predictive implications about the potential outcome for the economy and financial markets after the 2020 presidential election?**

To answer these critical questions, this book has been broken down into 15 chapters.

The Political Backdrop

The first four chapters of this book explore the political backdrop to the 2020 presidential election. In Chapter 1, I discuss why I wrote this book and how this third election book I have written carries over some themes from the 2016 and 2018 elections.

In Chapter 2, I discuss party choices and lack thereof. This includes a discussion of how primaries and caucuses are critical parts of what is ultimately a two-party system in American politics. Immediately thereafter, I examine some of the most important deciding factors of U.S. presidential elections: outcomes in so-called battleground states. It should be no surprise that Ohio and Florida are likely to be critical linchpins for a potential victor of the 2020 election.

In Chapter 4, I examine the political conditions ahead of the 2020 presidential election. And in Chapter 5, I examine an issue that is often discussed but seldom understood: political polarization. In the end, polarization has increased because it works. Courting a political base results in both votes and donations, leaving no question as to why ignoring the middle is often a core political strategy.

In Chapter 6, I look back at the midterm elections to see what implications we might glean from the dynamics of that hotly contested event and what data may provide insight into the outcome of the 2020 presidential election.

I noted that the single most important factor that is likely to impact the outcome of the 2020 election is the change in the unemployment rate between the midterm election and the presidential election.

I looked at countless data series, and the only financial or economic series that holds the most likely implications for the impact on the 2020 presidential election is the unemployment rate. Beyond the statistics of past elections, this also makes logical sense since people tend to vote with their feet. As such, I noted at the time that if the job market worsens relatively from the 2018 midterms until the presidential election in 2020, people will likely vote for someone other than the incumbent.

For now, the U.S. job market is strong. But if the unemployment rate remains low until election time, a Trump reelection would be consistent with historical data.

In Chapters 7 and 8, I examine the last two important political factors that impact most U.S. presidential elections. And both of these are linked: the importance of eyes on screens and the incumbent advantage.

In my discussion of eyes on screens, I explore the subject of advertising and campaigning spend — as well as the ability to get free airtime. This is also a notion that spills over into my discussion of the advantage incumbents have. After all, they can travel wherever they want, and they can draw media attention and a crowd at will — without spending valuable ad dollars.

The Economic and Financial Backdrop
In Chapters 9 and 10, I look at the economic and financial market conditions going into the 2020 election season.

Going into the 2016 U.S. presidential election, U.S. economic data had weakened. Business investment in the United States actually contracted in the end of 2015 and the beginning of 2016.

Some of the biggest exposures to the U.S. economy in 2016 stemmed from a few key sectors, including heavy industry, oil and gas, and finance. But despite these risks and exposures, overall U.S. economic growth was positive, with 2015 U.S. GDP at 2.9 percent and 2016 GDP at 1.6 percent.

In other words, the economy was pretty solid at the time of the 2016 presidential election. And the economy was even stronger at the time of the 2018 midterm elections.

Some of the downside risks to U.S. business investment seen in 2015 and 2016 are likely to come back to the front and center ahead of the 2020 presidential election as the stimulative economic effects of tax cuts have long faded — and trade risks have forced the global economy to slow sharply. Plus, some election uncertainty could also dampen business investment.

Fortunately, U.S. consumption is almost 70 percent of GDP. And people have jobs. Wages are also up. This means that even though the business side of the economy could slow sharply, a true recession would be difficult to imagine with the unemployment rate at a decades-low level of 3.6 percent.

These economic dynamics are the subject of Chapter 9. Of course, there is a big different between the state of the economy and the state of financial markets, which I discuss in Chapter 10.

Election Cyclicality

In Chapter 11, I discuss the historical relationship between the timing of presidential elections and the start of recessions over business cycles and elections since 1854.

In my analysis of election cyclicality, I have been most concerned with recession starts because the United States has been in its current business cycle expansion for a decade — since the Great Recession ended in June 2009. It's been the longest cycle in U.S. history, but that does not mean it will go on forever. This is why it was important to assess the potential timing and start of the next recession.

When targeting recession starts, I discovered a certain kind of *election cyclicality*, which has two main attributes related to how recessions and presidential elections coincide.

One attribute of election cyclicality is the election-recession window, which increases the odds of a recession starting shortly before or shortly after a U.S. presidential election. This has held true for all but one recession since the Great Depression. The second attribute is tied to a term limit on growth, which shows that there has never been a case of three full presidential terms without a recession starting. This has held true since 1854, which is as far back as we have U.S. economic and recession data.

Election-Recession Windows

As we look at the timing of recession starts, I present information about the narrow time frame in which recession starts happen, and how this has often occurred around presidential elections. It's something I call the *election-recession window*.

If we look back to all of the official recessions since 1854, we find that the election-recession window has actually narrowed since 1928. In other words, since the Great Depression, recessions have started closer to elections than before. Plus, there has only been one recession start since 1928 that did not occur in the 11 months leading up to a presidential election, or in the 13 months after a presidential election. This is a key part of the election-recession window — and we are quickly approaching it!

Term Limit on Growth

There are elections without recessions, but there have never been three consecutive presidential terms without a recession start. Never.

Since 1854, the historical maximum number of presidential terms without a recession start is two. There have been no exceptions. Think of it as a *term limit on growth*, which is the second attribute of election cyclicality.

This means that if we consider all of U.S. business cycle history, we are likely to see the next recession start before the end of Trump's current term. This dynamic would likely be the result of a few critical things that have changed for the U.S. economy in recent years.

First and foremost, the rise of the consumer as a more critical part of the U.S. economy is one of the factors that may short-circuit the historical evidence of election cyclicality. In my analysis of the historical relationship between elections and the start of recessions, there has never been a time when the U.S. economy expanded for three presidential terms. But unless a recession starts before December 2020, this would be a first. Of course, with such strong recent U.S. jobs data, I think that would also be understandable.

Financial and Economic Impacts
In Chapters 12 and 13, I discuss the economic and financial market and impacts of past presidential elections — and what it could mean for the economy and financial markets after the election.

Ahead of the 2018 midterm elections, I noted in *Midterm Economics* that we have experienced a very long economic cycle, and we escaped recession around the 2016 presidential election due to a massive surge in corporate optimism and business investment tied to expectations of a once-in-a-generation set of tax cuts. But the closer we get to the 2020 presidential election, the greater the odds of a recession.

Beyond the 2020 presidential election, long-term dynamics will be more critical for financial markets and the economy after the 2020 election. In the long run, equities and commodity prices tend to rise. The dollar also tends to weaken, generally, although that data has been asymmetrically impacted by the aftermath of Bretton Woods.

Risks to Growth and Markets

President Trump stated on 15 June 2019 that if he is not reelected it would trigger a "market crash the likes of which have not been seen before."[2] That is a very bold statement. And it is very likely going way too far.

But if the 2016 election showed us anything, it is that tax policy expectations have real and significant impacts on financial markets and the economy. In other words, if Trump wins, the odds are greater that the economy would likely remain on a more even keel, whereas if Trump loses, the short-term economic outlook will depend very much on the promised tax policies of the Democratic victor.

If there are promises of increased taxes, financial markets and business investment could take a really big hit. But if a Democrat with a probusiness agenda gets elected, it may be relatively benign or even positive for the U.S. economy, which has been slowing on weak global manufacturing and elevated trade risks that have been introduced by the Trump administration.

Long-Term Risks Unlikely to Change

As we look further into the future, there are bigger, major, long-term risks to the economy. These include the U.S. national debt, entitlement expenditures, demographics, and automation risks to the labor force. These are the focus of Chapter 14.

The good news is that some of these risks could be mitigated, if they were addressed. The bad news is that these risks were largely avoided during the 2016 presidential election.

This meant that President Trump was unlikely to address these risks, which threaten the American economy on an existential level. Furthermore, this eventuality was reinforced halfway through the current term by the fact that these risks were not considered or discussed in a significant way during the 2018 midterm elections.

Now, as we look ahead to the 2020 presidential election, it appears highly likely that whether the president that gets sworn in for the next presidential term is Trump or a Democrat contender, neither is likely to address these bigger, scarier things that are worse for the American economy.

These risks are big trains coming down the tracks toward a ravine without a bridge. And neither candidate is likely to build the bridge required. So it's up to you to prepare yourself!

This is the goal of Chapter 15, which comes after I discuss the big, long-term risks in Chapter 14. In fact, I dedicate Chapter 15 to helping you respond to these risks and challenges ahead.

Expectations for the 2020 Presidential Election

The 2020 election is 16 months away, and a lot can happen in that time. In President Trump's favor right now are his incumbency, his ability to get eyes on screens, and a strong economy. But if the unemployment rate rises, trade tensions cause growth to slow further, or some other unexpected events shift the voting dynamics of battleground states, he could be in for a fight that could be won by a not-yet-nominated Democratic challenger.

In the end, it should come as little surprise that the economic and financial market aftermath of the 2020 presidential election will be driven by tax policy expectations in the short run and by big, scary, unaddressed risks in the long run.

But before we get there, political polarization, weaponized social media, and subnational identities are likely to make the process an absolute shit-show — or, rather, a dumpster fire.

CHAPTER 1

WHY I WROTE THIS BOOK

In early 2018, I sat down with a Bloomberg reporter in New York City to discuss the analysis I was working on as part of my book *Midterm Economics*. The journalist requested the interview because the analysis I was conducting was original research.

You may wonder, what was I doing?

After all, one would think that since financial market and election data are all readily available, surely there couldn't be anything that new that I was working on.

But you would be wrong.

I was analyzing the historical impact of midterm elections on financial markets and the economy. And I was trying to identify if there were any economic indicators or financial markets that historically proved predictive of the outcome of the presidential election following the midterm election. Apparently, the research I was doing was exceptionally unique.

I wrote the book *Electing Recession* to take an objective look at financial market and economic data to see what implications could be drawn from the data. And I continued this process in *Midterm Economics*.

And apparently no one else had bothered to do this.

Before writing *Electing Recession*, I had conducted a search of analyses that were objective and took a financial market and economic perspective with respect to elections. Naturally, I did the same before writing *Midterm Economics*. Both times, I found nothing comparable. And it surprised me.

After all, I thought, if there are going to be countless talking heads going on Bloomberg, CNBC, MSNBC, Fox, CNN, and other news shows to talk about the election, had no one actually done any historical statistical analyses? Had no one tried to find financial market or economic patterns?

In this era of big data, it was surprising to me to have a journalist confirm that, indeed, no one was doing the kind of analysis I had performed in *Electing Recession* or that I was producing for the then-forthcoming book *Midterm Economics*.

No one was looking at actual numbers.

And this is one of the biggest problems with American politics. Everyone is so busy feeling certain ways about various issues, stirring up voters with emotional issues, or getting people glued into the news, that analysis and data fall by the wayside.

I wrote *The Dumpster Fire Election* to help you prepare for the potential impact of the coming U.S. election.

U.S. presidential elections are important for the economy and financial markets, which is why they get a lot of coverage in business media — and in general news media. And it's why there is often significant market commentary about elections written by financial analysts.

But even though people talk about how different candidates could impact the economy or financial markets, the fact that actual in-depth analysis of election data has not been conducted underscores the risk that such talk is often informed by political positions individuals hold rather than an objective analysis of the data.

When discussing the potential financial market and economic impact of the 2016 U.S. presidential election with others, I observed that people's sentiments about the economic impact of presidential candidates were often more visceral and emotional rather than based on an analysis of any kind of data. And the same was true going into the 2018 U.S. midterm elections.

Now, going into 2020, the rhetoric is likely to be dialed up even further. In an era of clickbait, fake news, biased reporting on both ends of the political spectrum, and over-democratization of opinion that makes anyone (or any entity) on social media a full-on media pundit, there is a greater need than ever for actual analysis. There is a need to look at numbers and trendlines that go beyond the headlines.

It's one thing to talk about data and to have a feeling about a candidate, but it is a very different thing to actually look at the historical data objectively to identify trends. Simply put, it's more difficult, and it's something that's been done infrequently — and often with a political bent.

I have tried very hard in this book to present numbers as they are, not how I (or anyone else) would like them to be.

Objectivity, Correlation, and Causality

When I started working on my election trilogy, my mind was a complete blank slate in terms of expectations. That was as true when I was writing *Electing Recession* and *Midterm Economics* as it was in writing *The Dumpster Fire Election*. What you'll read in this book about the results of my analysis was initially a surprise to me, and it might be a surprise for you too.

Before I had written a word of *Electing Recession*, I knew two things. First, I knew that this kind of analysis had not been performed in this way before. Second, I knew that the data was going to show something cool. I wasn't sure what I was going to find, but I was pretty sure it would be interesting. In the end, the results of analyzing past presidential elections were exceptionally interesting, and they made *Electing Recession* a bestseller.

Going into *Midterm Economics*, I knew pretty much the same thing. I knew analysis was lacking — and that something important would come out of it. This made launching the book at the Council on Foreign Relations in 2018 very exciting.

The most important result was to show that the change in the unemployment rate between the midterm and presidential elections has historically been be the single most critical factor in determining the outcome of the subsequent presidential election.

So, Why Me?

I have spent the past 15 years of my career analyzing economic, financial market, and political data. I hold a master's in economics and this is now my third book about elections, economics, and financial markets. In the time that I've been a professional business economist, I've analyzed data about the economy, commodity markets, foreign exchange rates, interest rates, the oil and gas industry, the metals industry, automotive parts and vehicle manufacturing, and material handling. And I've been ranked a top forecaster in the world by Bloomberg News in 43 different categories since 2011 for the accuracy of my forecasts in those areas. I see a lot of new data all the time, and the one thing I can tell you is that every time I see new data, there are surprises.

Sometimes the data shows you what you expect, but other times the data shows you something wild. My analysis of historical recession data is a mix of mild and wild, as you will see.

Implications extrapolated from data can be very important because they can impact investment decisions and business strategic planning, and they can impact you personally. In the chapters ahead, I present the potential near-term and medium-term economic and financial market implications of the 2020 U.S. presidential election.

No Axe to Grind

I'm not Glenn Beck, Ann Coulter, or James Carville. I'm not a political pundit, and I don't have an axe to grind in this book against one party or the other. This isn't to say that I do not have biases. Of course I do. But when I wrote this book (and my last two election books), I did the analysis first. Furthermore, I pride myself on writing without partisan views, and I am honored to be a member of two important nonpartisan organizations in Texas.

The first nonpartisan organization is the Texas Business Leadership Council, which is the business roundtable for the state of Texas. Comprised of only 100 members, it is the only CEO-led public policy organization in the state of Texas that advises state and federal elected leadership on important economic issues that help foster a more globally competitive Texas. As part of the TBLC's Federal Issues Task Force, I made trips in March 2018 and in June 2019 to Capitol Hill to meet with Texas elected officials on issues related to trade, the replacement of NAFTA, and the USMCA. My experiences on those trips and in those closed-door discussions have informed some of my political and economic expectations.

The second nonpartisan organization in Texas that I am a member of is the Texas Lyceum. Founded almost 40 years ago to support the advancement of Texas as a third coast of economic and political thought, the Lyceum is founded on the Aristotelian model of business and political discourse. It is also the preeminent nonpartisan leadership development organization and the most trusted venue for nonpartisan discourse in Texas.

Most impressively, the demographics of the Lyceum mirror almost exactly the population in the state of Texas — by party, gender, race, regional origin, religion, and sexual orientation. There is also a diverse representation of members by profession, although there is a very high percentage of civil servants, budding politicians, government officials, and lawyers.

I'm in it for the civil bipartisan discourse.

As you can hopefully tell, I am an analyst to the core. And I believe that there are a number of issues that are more critical than party. These include the health of the economy, national wealth, the job market, and financial markets.

After all, who doesn't want to see a healthy economy? Who doesn't want to see people with jobs? Who doesn't want to see solid and stable financial markets?

I think these are generally bipartisan goals that everyone can agree on. It's part of the reason why Fed appointments have remained generally less politicized than in almost any other organization in the United States. Because the Fed's mandate is to support full employment and keep inflation low but stable, near the 2 percent level.

Generally speaking, these are solid goals of both parties, their members, their constituents, and the U.S. population in general. Along those lines, my analysis in *The Dumpster Fire Election* looks at some of the unfortunate social fraying that likely lies ahead as well as the potential impact on the economy and markets.

It is this mix of nonpartisan perspective and statistical focus that I bring to the table. It's why I wrote this book. And it's an extension of the work I have been building on since 2016.

Be Prepared, Whoever Wins

This book provides an objective look at recent U.S. presidential elections and presidencies, to glean from them some insights into what the outcome of the 2020 presidential election might hold for the economy and financial markets. Equally important, however, is the question "What is unlikely to change no matter which candidate is elected?"

Whether we end up with the second term of an incumbent Donald Trump or a Democratic challenger, I want you to be prepared for the potential outcomes — based on the numbers. You may not be happy with the outcome in terms of who you want to see elected president, but maybe you can be prepared. Some things are unlikely to differ much regardless of the candidate and party of the next president. And some of those things are good. But some of them are very bad.

This is not a book about the history of American politics, although I have included the first section of this book to help set the stage for our discussion. After all, even before we dig into the current economic situation or the intersection of politics and economics, I need to share a brief overview of the historical and current political dynamics in the United States. For U.S. political aficionados, this section is likely to seem somewhat rudimentary, but this information will help outline the political landscape and battlefield ahead of the 2020 election.

I think this is an important section because, especially for foreign readers or those who do not happen to be deeply steeped in politics, this should provide some fundamental background information.

Based on my analysis in *Electing Recession*, U.S. presidential elections may actually be more important than previously expected for the economy. It's important to look at how U.S. economic indicators like unemployment, industrial production, and GDP growth respond to different parties holding the reins of power, as well as to presidential elections in general.

Correlation and Causation

I have tried to share my analysis in this book as objectively as possible.

In a presentation I gave back in 2016, I shared my analysis showing that unemployment rates had fallen for every Democratic president since the end of World War II except Carter, and that unemployment rates had risen for every Republican president except Reagan.

One executive quickly jumped in: "Republican unemployment rates rise because Republican presidents follow Democrats, and Democrat rates fall, because they follow Republicans!" While this is not a completely accurate representation of presidential term sequence, it does underscore a very important issue: the correlation of historical data are not necessarily indicative of causality. I will talk about this more when I get to the topic of unemployment and other U.S. economic data in Chapter 12.

This Time is Different

When people think about the financial impact of elections, there is a tendency for analysts on Wall Street and observers on Main Street to focus almost exclusively on equity markets.

This book is different because it takes a look at equity markets *and* economic indicators, currency rates, oil prices, and precious metals prices. Of course, as you will see, some data and markets can be greatly influenced by the outcome of presidential elections, while others have trended independently. The ramifications of presidential elections for the economy and financial markets have not been looked at previously in such an intercorrelated market framework.

I find this kind of cross-market approach to be very helpful in my regular market forecasting as the President and Chief Economist of Prestige Economics.

It's worked out well so far, and Bloomberg News has ranked me a top forecaster in 43 different categories for my forecast accuracy since 2011. These rankings have been awarded for my accuracy in predicting economic indicators, foreign exchange rates, energy prices, metals prices, and agricultural prices. I remain convinced that looking beyond equity markets produces some unique, high-value insights that most analysts otherwise miss.

There is also one thing in this book that is very different than the last two election books I penned.

Both *Midterm Economics* and *Electing Recession* were released during election years. *Midterm Economics* was released in June 2018, while *Electing Recession* was released in August 2016. If I were tracking with historical calendars, this book should not be out for another year.

But I wanted this book to come out sooner. I wanted to help foster discussion around real issues related to financial markets and the economy as well as encourage discourse related to some of the foundational issues that could make this election turn into an absolute dumpster fire. I wanted to call early attention to the still-elevated risks around manipulation of social media messaging, political polarization, and the risky acceleration in subnational identities that threaten a cohesive national identity and that could fracture society more and more with each important national election.

There's actually a lot more at stake in the 2020 presidential election than the economy, financial markets, or even who wins.

In the long run, the biggest risks stem from underfunded entitlements.

But right now, the biggest threats from the 2020 presidential election stem from how the election is waged by both sides.

And with that, we are off to the dumpster fire!

CHAPTER 2

PARTY CHOICES
AND LACK THEREOF

A lot of attention is paid in the early days of an election campaign to how many candidates are running for president. And this year is likely to be no exception, with 20 Democratic candidates set to participate in debates that require two parts in Miami at the end of June 2019.

But even though the horde of candidates catches the eye, by the time the election actually happens, American voters will only have two real choices.

Two Parties, Winner Takes All
The political system in the United States is a winner-take-all voting system that favors two parties. There are other parties, but there are only two political parties that have a shot at winning the presidency in 2020: Republicans and Democrats. The dominating parties have changed over time, but these are the main two now.

Of course, there are other parties beyond these two major parties. According to ballotpedia.org, about 30 other political parties participated in the 2016 presidential election.

Three of these minor parties were recognized in more than 10 states: the Libertarian Party (33 states), the Green Party (21 states), and the Constitution Party (13 states).[1] There may be a lot of parties, but because of the winner-take-all nature of the U.S. voting system, the final presidential contest comes down to an election between these two main party candidates.

The *de facto* two-party system has generally been the reality since the election of 1796, which followed George Washington's unanimous elections in 1789 and 1792.

In other words, other than for the election of the first president of the United States, most elections have been between two main parties.[2] There have been third parties at times, but the winner-take-all system favors consolidation to two parties. Of course, the natures of the two main U.S. political parties — Republican and Democrat — have evolved and changed over time, as have their platforms, voter bases, and core values on critical issues like slavery, abolition, civil rights, and isolationism. The parties have changed over time, but the number of main parties has not. For most of American history, there have been two main players. That's a product of a winner-take-all voting system.

If we look for presidents that identified as Democrats, Andrew Jackson was the first modern Democratic president. And he was first elected president in 1828.[3] The first Republican president was Abraham Lincoln, who was first elected president in 1860.

Primaries and Caucuses

In their modern incarnations, U.S. political parties push a nominated candidate forward in the race to the White House through a funneling process that involves primaries and caucuses, in which the parties each elect a nominee ahead of the general election. In order to narrow down which politician becomes his or her party champion, the party members must have an election before the election. The culmination of this process occurs at party conventions.

Sometimes it seems like everyone wants to be president — or at least it seems like every politician does!

Ahead of the 2016 election, there were initially 17 main Republican candidates — so many, in fact, that for a number of the debates between the candidates, there had to be two separate stages.

As for the Democrats, there were five main candidates registered in 2016, but only two won delegates, Bernie Sanders and Hillary Clinton. Going into the 2020 presidential election season, there are 20 candidates that will appear at the first Democratic debates.

While there are a slew of Democrats vying for the Democratic nomination, there are unlikely to be any serious Republican challengers to Donald Trump. Trump is wildly likely to receive the Republican nomination because there has only been one time when a sitting president did not receive the party nomination, and it was Franklin Pierce. He was a Democrat and the 14th president of the United States.[4]

Four other presidents did not receive their party nomination, but none of those four was elected in his own right.[5]

In other words, not only has only one elected president not received his party's nomination for reelection, but there have been zero times that a Republican who was elected for president was not nominated for reelection.

Given the consistent historical pattern of nominated incumbents and the current state of the U.S. economy, the prospects of Trump's renomination seem exceptionally high.

Furthermore, presidential candidates for reelection who face a significant challenger have a much lower chance of being reelected. In fact, no sitting president has survived a serious primary challenge.[6]

But given how Trump handily dispatched the other 16 serious Republican party contenders in 2016, no serious challenger seems likely to emerge to challenge him. For this reason as well, the prospects of Trump's second term are likely to be undiminished.

Conventions, Primaries, and Caucuses

There are two ways that voters in the two main political parties decide which candidate will be the nominee for president. They vote in primaries and caucuses, in which the candidates collect delegates, which are awarded based on victories in those primaries and caucuses.

There are also superdelegates in each party. These are party insiders whose votes are not tied to any specific primary or caucus outcome.

Once the primaries and caucuses have been concluded in all 50 states, Washington, D.C., and U.S. territories, the parties hold a convention, where a candidate is officially nominated.

One major downside of the primary and caucus system is that it can create internal party strife and conflict. And this can also provide ammunition for the opposing party's candidate during the general election. This strife is a key reason why a sitting president is often not reelected if there is a contentious primary.

Ahead of the 2016 election, both parties found themselves dealing with internal challenges to the candidates they would ultimately nominate for president. The Republican party had a very contentious primary season and found itself quite divided as Donald Trump, a political outsider with a large personality, clinched the nomination. Republicans going into this election now find themselves with a Hobson's choice.

A Lot Can Change

There is one final thing to consider about the 2020 presidential election when it comes to primaries and caucuses: a lot can change from the beginning of the election season until the end.

Right now, there are 20 main Democratic candidates who are set to take the stage in Miami at the end of June 2019 for the first candidate debate. And the election is over 16 months away!

To put this in perspective, let's look back at who some of the leading candidates were at this time in the past four elections.

In a Gallup poll from June 2003, the leader of the Democratic field going into the 2004 election season was Joe Lieberman, who was favored by 20 percent of poll respondents.[7] Kerry ultimately got the nomination.

Going into the 2008 election season, Gallup polls conducted in June 2007 showed that Hillary Clinton was the leading Democratic party candidate and Rudy Giuliani was the leading Republican party candidate.[8] Obama and McCain ultimately got the nominations.

Ahead of the 2012 presidential election, Gallup polls showed Romney as the leader in June 2011.[9] He ultimately got the Republican party nomination.

In April 2015, Rubio led a Quinnipiac University poll as the Republican front-runner.[10] But in June 2015, Trump led the pack in a Gallup poll as the "best-known" candidate, although Rubio had the highest "net favorable" score.[11] Hillary Clinton, however, was an early leader for the Democratic party nomination.[12]

There is a pattern over the contested (nonincumbent) party nominations over the past four presidential elections and the leader this far out: the odds do not favor the early leader.

In total, only two of the six competitive primary leaders this early got the nomination.

Romney (in 2012) and Clinton (in 2016) were the only candidates who clearly led this far out in a contested field and who also ultimately received their party nominations.

Because he is the incumbent and because he easily dispatched the other Republican challengers leading up to the 2016 presidential election, Trump is unlikely to face a serious challenger and should secure the Republican party nomination with ease. But, the outlook for the Democrats is quite different.

By the Numbers

Joe Biden is leading the pack right now,[13] but clinching the nomination is far from a fait accompli for the candidate. Both he and Bernie Sanders have one thing in common that presents a significant challenge to their candidacies: their age. Biden will be 77 at the time of the 2016 election,[14] and Sanders will be 79 at the time of the election.[15]

While both of these candidates are popular, there is a practical side of waging party-organized elections. And the biggest practical consideration is that a party will ideally want to back a candidate who could be elected and then subsequently reelected so that the party can hold the office of the president for eight years. After all, competitive primaries are also very expensive, because candidates are funded who will ultimately not face the opposing party's nominee in the actual election. And having an incumbent allows a party to focus its funding on the incumbent, rather than a field of almost countless candidates.

Constitutionally, the minimum age to be president is 35.

There is no maximum.

But Democratic party superdelegates who can significantly impact the outcome of the primaries and the ultimate nomination may favor a candidate that would not be an octogenarian at the time of a potential future reelection.

After all, the Democratic donors, super PACs, and party fundraisers want to make a smart decision with the biggest chance of success over the longest period of time possible.

If the Democratic primaries look like they will be close, I would expect party leaders to favor a younger candidate to maximize the return on the massive political capital that will be expended in the 2020 Democratic primaries and general election.

This isn't to say that Biden wouldn't be reelectable at age 81 or that Sanders wouldn't be reelectable at age 83, but these are theories that I suspect much of the Democratic party would prefer not to test.

And it is something potential Democratic donors are also wary of.

Voting From the Holy Roman Empire or *Game of Thrones*

After the Democratic and Republican party conventions, candidates begin to focus on the coming presidential election. Presidents capture the White House, however, not by winning total popular votes but by amassing electoral votes. Like in the Holy Roman Empire, electors chose the leader.

It's also no longer a spoiler to point out that this is not too dissimilar to the leadership voting structure put in place at the end of the show *Game of Thrones.*

The group of U.S. electors is called the Electoral College, and they are apportioned to the states and Washington, D.C. in a similar manner as the congressional power of each state.

Each state receives one electoral vote for each congressman and senator from that state. Plus, three additional electoral votes are allocated to Washington, D.C., making the total number of electors 538 (100 senators, 435 congressmen, and 3 D.C. electors).[16]

The democratic part of this process kicks in when the electors usually (but are not required to) cast their votes for the presidential candidate that wins their state — or district, in the case of Washington, D.C. Usually these votes are allocated as winner-take-all, but there are exceptions.

There are a few different reasons why the system works this way, and both of these reasons harken back to the founding of the original 13 United States. The structure of the elector system was designed to prevent the direct election of a president by the people, as a safeguard against populists.

Plus, the allocation of electoral votes was structured to balance the concerns of smaller states against the will of larger states, which also explains our bicameral allocation of votes mirrored by the Electoral College.

Election Background Review

Let's review a few important takeaways from this chapter.

First, U.S. politics has historically been dominated by two parties because of the U.S. winner-take-all system of voting. The two current dominant parties are the Democrats and the Republicans. Each of the two main political parties goes through its own independent voting process, using primaries and caucuses, to nominate a candidate to represent the party in the run for the U.S. presidency. The parties want to ideally nominate someone who could easily serve two terms as president, which could prove to be a disadvantage for candidates in their late 70s, like Joe Biden and Bernie Sanders.

In the end, party loyalists will have a Hobson's choice when it comes to the candidate that gets the nomination. There is only one candidate per party that gets a nomination for the presidential election. And to underscore how important these nominations are, only 9 percent of Americans chose Hillary Clinton or Donald Trump in 2016.[17]

The U.S. president is chosen by electors, not by a directly democratic election process. The electors are apportioned in similar lines to congressional representation for each of the states. Electors may, but are not required to, vote for the presidential candidate who wins their state. The District of Columbia also gets three electors, although it is not a state.

Now that we've gone over some of the basics, let's talk about battleground states!

CHAPTER 3

THE IMPORTANCE OF BATTLEGROUND STATES

Presidential candidates have to win electoral votes in the general election that are apportioned by state, rather than by the overall popular vote. As such, they focus on the states that can get them the biggest bang for the buck. Some states have a history of consistently and reliably voting for one party or the other, and they get less attention during the campaigning season. The biggest attention goes to the states that could potentially land in either camp. These states are called swing states — or battleground states.

Because of modern historical voting patterns, the chessboard of a presidential election in the United States is set well in advance. And it hinges very much on the outcome of these swing states.

In 2016, 99 percent of 2016 presidential campaign spending was in battleground states. The two most important fronts were Ohio and Florida. But Pennsylvania and North Carolina also garnered much attention in the 2016 presidential election, 71 percent of campaign spending was in just those four states as you can see in Figure 3-1.[1]

The Most Critical Battleground States: Ohio and Florida

While a rise in the unemployment rate could stack the deck against a Trump reelection in 2020 and other celebrity candidates could enter the election field, battleground states will still be important. And the two most important battleground states are Ohio and Florida.

They have high levels of electoral votes, and they have been critical for determining the outcome of many U.S. presidential elections. They have been, however, more critical to ensuring Republican victories.

Figure 3-1: Spending in Swing States[2]

99% of Presidential Campaign Spending is in Battleground States

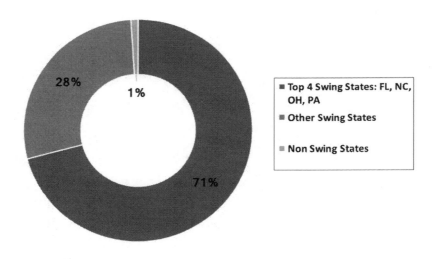

- Top 4 Swing States: FL, NC, OH, PA
- Other Swing States
- Non Swing States

Source: Analysis of Associated Press data by Nonprofit VOTE, Prestige Economics LLC

PRESTIGE ECONOMICS

1) For Democrats, Ohio is critical.

The last Democrat to be voted into office without winning Ohio was JFK in 1960. And even though there are 20 Democratic candidates that will take the stage in Miami at the end of June, I think you would be hard-pressed to find even a Democratic party leader who would say there is a JFK in the bunch. This means that the ultimate Democratic nominee will very likely need to win Ohio to become president.

2) For Republicans, Ohio is even more critical.

The last time a Republican won the presidential election without winning Ohio was...never. That's right. There have been exactly zero times that a Republican has become president without winning Ohio. The first Republican victory in Ohio dates back to 1860, with Abraham Lincoln, and the importance of Ohio is likely to remain high for the foreseeable future.

3) For Republicans, Florida is critical, although it is somewhat less important for Democrats.

The last Republican to win the White House without winning Florida was Calvin Coolidge in 1924. So it would be a key state for the Trump campaign to win.

2020 Preview Summary

If a candidate wants to be president, they must win battleground states. Both Democratic and Republican campaigns are likely to focus on Florida and Ohio as states where a lot of the advertising budget — and face time — needs to be spent. I expect the 2020 presidential campaign spending will look similar to the spending in 2016, with a clear focus on battleground states.

Meanwhile, the economic backdrop will be important for determining the next presidential election, as will the celebrity status of the candidates.

But for either party, securing as many battleground states as possible will be critical. I made the same arguments going into the 2016 presidential election about the importance of Florida and Ohio as I do today. And it proved prescient.

These two states, above all, are likely to remain critical bellwethers of the 2020 election season ahead. And they will very likely be the critical deciding factors of victory.

CHAPTER 4

POLITICAL CONDITIONS AHEAD OF THE 2020 ELECTION

While Democrats put a lot of weight and hope on the outcome of the midterm elections, I warned in *Midterm Economics* that even significant wins could prove part of a pyrrhic victory. Because there was a risk that changes might only occur at the margin — with some of the greatest risks to the U.S. economy unlikely to be tempered or mitigated by the midterm election outcome.

The midterm elections were a big win for Democrats in the House, although the Republican party maintained control of the Senate as we expected.

Going into the 2020 U.S. presidential election season, political tensions and polarization are high. And Democrats, after having generally "won" the 2018 midterms, are looking to win in 2020.

A backdrop of a strong economy, incessant political scandals, and investigations have been permanent fixtures of the Trump administration. Media polarization and social media toxicity have only strengthened as drivers of subnational identity that could make emotions run high this election season.

And the start of the election season is here. Around the time of this book's publication, the Democrats will be having their first debate in Miami. So the candidates are off to the races!

Unlike *Electing Recession* and *Midterm Economics*, *The Dumpster Fire Election* is being released earlier. As such, the path to nominee is less clear. There are 20 contenders that will be on the dais for the debate — or rather for the two different debates — at the end of June 2019.[1]

This means the conflict is about to ramp up. Big time!

An article in *The Atlantic* from 10 June 2019 titled "The Democratic Clown Car Rolls Into Iowa" hit the right notes.[2] Because the field of candidates is crowded to almost a crazy level. And the fight for the Democratic party nomination, which starts in Iowa, will be a tough one.

And so will the fight for the presidency.

There was a powerful — if not exaggerated — article on the topic of U.S. political divisiveness that was released during the 2016 political season. In the July/August issue of *The Atlantic*, Jonathan Rauch penned the piece titled "How American Politics Went Insane."[3]

Although the article was about the 2016 election season, Rauch opens up with an as-yet unrealized dystopian view of what the 2020 presidential election season might look like.

The outlook Rauch shares, which includes Trump serving only one term, has not come to pass.

Trump is running for reelection. And his chances look good.

After all, the economy is in good shape, and the outcome of the presidential election will be determined by electoral votes and eyes on screens — topics that I address in the following chapters.

But one part of Rauch's article still rings true. The elevated political polarization seen in 2016 was not just a one-off event. And it may be merely a preview of the chaos to come.

Rauch notes that in 2016, Jeb Bush called Trump a "chaos candidate." Rauch also notes that "Trump, however, didn't cause the chaos. The chaos caused Trump. What we are seeing is not a temporary spasm of chaos but a chaos *syndrome*."[4]

Rauch then goes on to define chaos syndrome and what it means for the U.S. political system and the U.S. government:

> Chaos syndrome is a chronic decline in the political system's capacity for self-organization. It begins with the weakening of the institutions and brokers — political parties, career politicians, and congressional leaders and committees — that have historically held politicians accountable to one another and prevented everyone in the system from pursuing naked self-interest all the time. As these intermediaries' influence fades, politicians, activists, and voters all become more individualistic and unaccountable. The system atomizes. Chaos becomes the new normal — both in campaigns and in the government itself.[5]

From Russia With Chaos

Despite talk to the contrary, a lot of the chaos in 2016 didn't just stem from problems within the U.S. political system. A great deal of chaos was delivered courtesy of Russian interference in the U.S. elections. This is just one level of the weaponization of social media. And the Russians did it in a big way.

According to the U.S. indictment of Internet Research Organization, LLC — the vehicle through which Russians interfered in the U.S. 2016 presidential election — the Russians had "a *monthly* budget of approximately $1.25 million toward interference efforts by September 2016 and that it employed 'hundreds of individuals for its online operation.'"[6]

Furthermore, Nate Silver noted that according to the indictment, "the interference campaign had been underway for years (since at least 2014) and gradually evolved from a more general-purpose trolling operation into something that sought to undermine Clinton while promoting Trump (and to a lesser degree, Bernie Sanders). To the extent it mattered, it would have blended into the background and had a cumulative effect over the entirety of the campaign."[7]

So what was the total visibility? In total, 126 million users on Facebook saw Russian messaging as well as those who saw the more than 131,000 messages on Twitter and the more than 1,000 videos on YouTube.[8]

Looking at the actual impact of social media virality is not a new challenge.

It's something companies grapple with every day. But there is one thing that seems certain, as in all advertising: the more people see a message, the greater the impact.

In comparison to the funds Clinton and Trump dedicated to the election — or the number of staffers — the amount spent by Internet Research Organization, LLC is a relatively small number. But these funds were spent in Russia, where the funds can go a lot further. Silver also noted that "the Russian efforts were on the small side as compared with the massive magnitudes of the campaigns, but not so small that you'd consider them a rounding error." Silver also noted that "Clinton was viewed as dishonest and untrustworthy" because the Russian campaign used hashtags like #Hillary4Prison."[9]

Forensic accountants have been able to trace how cryptocurrencies, for example, were used to pay for some of the Russian interference. And while that is helpful ex post facto, it may not help stop future interference. Especially if Facebook and other social media that were compromised in an influencer way to unduly influence the election are intent on continuing to keep the ill-gotten goods earned in the process. In other words, if Facebook continues to keep the money from politically subversive campaigns, how can we possibly expect that this will in any way incentivize a true change in behavior?

To wit, I would highly recommend the eye-opening article from *Vice News* appropriately titled, "We posed as 100 Senators to run ads on Facebook. Facebook approved all of them." The article exposed how easy it was for *Vice News* to post approved "paid for by" ads for all 100 senators in October 2018.[10]

The conclusion of the *Vice News* exposé was that "the 'Paid for by' feature is easily manipulated and appears to allow anyone to lie about who is paying for a political ad, or to pose as someone paying for the ad."[11] And this was as recent as October 2018!

Subnational Identity

One of the biggest issues with the social media campaigns of foreign interference, as well as with social media in general, is that it fosters subnational identity.

Benedict Anderson was a professor of international studies at Cornell University and one of the most respected theorists of nationalism. He argued in *Imagined Communities* that nationalism is artificial and contingent on fostering the improbable notion that a group of varied, disjointed individuals have something in common with one another and that this common denominator is "nationalism."

Anderson presents the notion of the nation as an imagined community in terms of a shared language and common literary history and daily national interaction fostered through newspapers. For Anderson, justification for nationalism lies in linguistic unity and is the direct result of the rampant primacy of print capitalism.

Anderson states that "what, in a positive sense, made the new communities imaginable was a half-fortuitous, but explosive interaction between a system of production and productive relations (capitalism), a technology of communications (print), and the fatality of human linguistic diversity."[12]

Anderson's book first appeared in 1983, long before the advent of social media. But it was a major part of the master's thesis I wrote in 2001, and Anderson's theories still ring true today.

After all, social media is the current form of print capitalism. Let's call it *digital print capitalism*. There is perhaps no better way to describe it. After all, for all of the paid Russian interference on social media, Facebook and the others kept all the money. There was no attempt to create a foundation or fund to protect or preserve democracy. It wasn't even an afterthought.

Furthermore, it is through that bought-and-paid-for lens of digital print capitalism that people develop their own identities. And these identities are no longer linked by a geographic frame of reference as in the nationalist print capitalism of yore.

No, today's digital print capitalism creates and reinforces attitudes and identities that have no borders and know no regions but that are still linked by linguistic similarities. But the language that binds today is not merely that of a nation-state. The language that is used to bind and divide people today is very much dialed into value signaling. It is fostered by a corporate push to identity prime avatars, target customers, and likely members of voter groups.

In truth, if it's your mother's birthday and you wish her a happy birthday on Facebook, you'll see a little more of your mother. But if you hate cats and someone posts about cats and you engage with the platform to write a long diatribe about how much you hate cats, you're going to see a whole lot more about cats!

Every time there is a new Hello Kitty or Pusheen toy, a popular cat video, or even a *Cats* revival, you'll see it.

I realize this sounds a bit extreme. But the truth is that content platforms like Facebook want you to engage. And a platform shows you things you will engage with because it wants eyes on screens to sell you things. This means that you will see things you love and things you hate.

This kind of platform has proven to be fruitful ground for fostering identity politics. And this reinforces identity in a way that print capitalism did on a national scare at the fin de siècle. The big difference is that you can have very tiny segmented groups of identity that are exposed to constant articles and online content that reinforce the notion that they are not alone — that their identity, whatever it may be, is essentially the dominant identity, the only identity, or even the right identity.

The efficacy of the primacy of digital print capitalism has an analog historical equivalent: Anderson's primacy of print capitalism. And it means that this time is not different. It may be digital, but we have seen how this plays out before. And it means that more conflict lies ahead — not just during election season, but potentially on a pervasive and persistent basis for society.

In the next chapter, we'll take a look at why polarization is so important in American politics. And we will look at some data that underscores how social media interactions are playing out between Americans with different political leanings.

CHAPTER 5

POLITICAL POLARIZATION

Why is American politics becoming more polarized?

The answer is simple: because it works.

According to research by the Pew Research Center, voters who are consistently conservative or consistently liberal are more likely to vote — and they are more likely to donate.

In other words, if you want to win and you want to raise funds, you need to court those with consistent views at one end of the political spectrum — or the other. You can see this breakdown in Figure 5-1, which shows that 78 percent of those who are "consistently conservative" always vote. This compares starkly to the 39 percent of "mixed" party affiliation voters who always vote.[1] In other words, consistent conservatives are exactly twice as likely to always vote as moderates. This is why rhetoric doesn't target moderates. They won't always vote.

So why bother with messaging to the middle?

This kind of partisan-supporting dynamic can also be seen in fundraising.

In the same Pew report, and in Figure 5-1, you can see that 31 percent of consistently liberal voters reported contributing to political candidates or groups "in the past two years."[2]

This compares to the only 8 percent of voters with "mixed" political spectrum affiliation.[3] This means consistently liberal people are almost four times more likely to donate to a political candidate than those with mixed views. At the other end of the spectrum, consistently conservative voters were over three times more likely to donate to a political candidate than those with mixed views.

Again, why bother with the middle? This data clearly shows why candidates don't really market to the mixed middle. After all, there's no votes in it and there is no fundraising in it. The ends of the political spectrum are much more mobilized — and ready to spend to support their views.

Additional research from Pew further highlighted a move to the ends of the political spectrum over a 20 year period. Between 1994 and 2014, the combined 10 percent of voters at the ends of the political spectrum more than doubled to 21 percent of voters. Meanwhile, the mixed middle fell from 49 percent to 39 percent during that same time period. You can see this dynamic in Figure 5-2.[4]

Figure 5-1: Votes and Donations at the Ends of the Spectrum[5]

Political Activism Gap: Right and Left More Likely to Vote, Donate to Campaigns

 *Percent who **always vote***

 *Percent who contributed to a **political candidate or group** in the past two years*

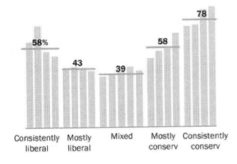

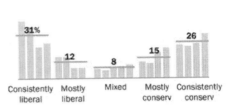

Source: 2014 Political Polarization in the American Public
Note: Bars represent the level of participation at each point on an ideological consistency scale of 10 political values questions. Figures are reported on the five ideological consistency groups used throughout the report (see Appendix A).

PEW RESEARCH CENTER

Figure 5-2: The Shrinking Mixed Middle[6]

Growing Minority Holds Consistent Ideological Views

On a 10-item scale of political values, % who are...

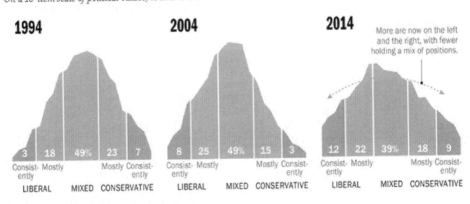

Source: 2014 Political Polarization in the American Public
Notes: Ideological consistency based on a scale of 10 political values questions. (See Appendix A for details on how the scale is constructed and how scores are grouped.)

PEW RESEARCH CENTER

In addition to votes and fundraising incentivizing political polarization at the ends of the political spectrum, there has been a significant shift over a 20-year period of Democrats being more consistently liberal and Republicans being more consistently conservative.[7]

In Figure 5-3, you can see how the distribution of voters has become more "consistently" liberal and conservative between 1994 and 2014.

Figure 5-3: Polarization of Views Over 20 Years[8]

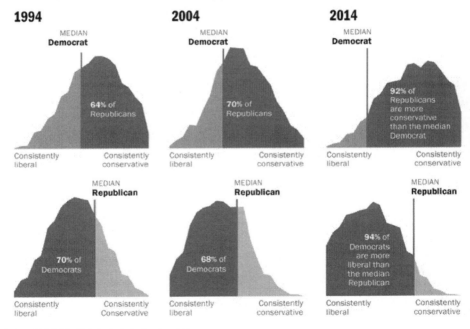

Republicans Shift to the Right, Democrats to the Left

Distribution of Republicans and Democrats on a 10-item scale of political values

Source: 2014 Political Polarization in the American Public
Notes: Ideological consistency based on a scale of 10 political values questions (see Appendix A). Republicans include Republican-leaning independents; Democrats include Democratic-leaning independents (see Appendix B).

PEW RESEARCH CENTER

There are other dynamics that vary by party as well. In a separate study, the Pew foundation noted that consistent liberals were more likely to drop a friend because of their political views, whereas consistent conservatives are more likely to have close friends who share their political views.[9]

But while there may be difference as to how conservatives and liberals manage their friend cohorts with respect to politics, one thing seems to be clear: antipathy is on the rise for both parties.

In Figure 5-4, you can see how both Democrats and Republicans have developed increased levels of antipathy for each other over time. This is especially true for the percentage who view each other "very unfavorably" more than it is for those who view each other merely "unfavorably."

Figure 5-4: Votes and Donations at Ends of Spectrum[10]

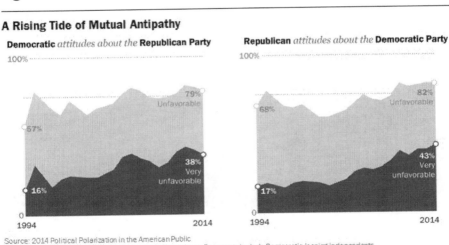

A Rising Tide of Mutual Antipathy

Democratic *attitudes about the* Republican Party

Republican *attitudes about the* Democratic Party

Source: 2014 Political Polarization in the American Public
Note: Republicans include Republican-leaning independents; Democrats include Democratic-leaning independents.

PEW RESEARCH CENTER

The media dynamics are also challenging in the United States as well. In a recent Reuters study, the online news media polarization was scored across countries. Polarization of the media in the United States was the highest by far — and it was twice as high as most European countries. You can see this in Figure 5-5.

In short, money and votes flow from a polarized populace. And the media is all too happy to play along with this polarization, whether it be traditional, online, or social media. These are some of the critical ingredients to an increasingly toxic political environment — and the perfect storm to light up a social and political dumpster fire.

Figure 5-5: Online Media Polarization[11]

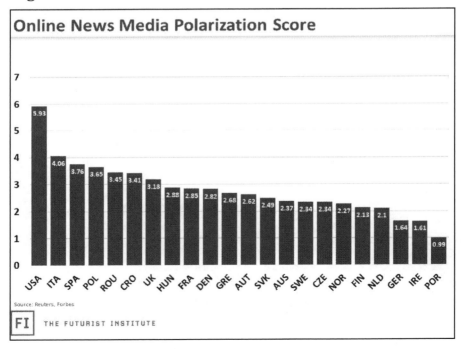

CHAPTER 6

MIDTERM ELECTION
IMPLICATIONS FOR 2020

There have only been 12 one-term presidents in the history of the United States, with only three in the last hundred years: Carter, George H. W. Bush, and Hoover. In addition to these presidents, some people also consider Ford a one-term president since he replaced Nixon and ran for reelection — but he lost.

In all four of those instances — Carter, Bush, Hoover, and Ford — the U.S. unemployment rate was higher in the month before the presidential election than it had been during the November of the prior midterm election. This did not occur for any of the first terms of other U.S. presidents since 1930.

All of these increases, except for under Hoover, can be seen in Figure 6-1. The unemployment rate rose abysmally under Hoover during the Great Depression, from 3.2 percent at the end of 1930 (the year of the midterm election) to 16.9 percent by the end of 1932 (the year of the next presidential election).[1]

Implications for the 2020 Presidential Election

Since the U.S. unemployment rate was near historically low levels in May 2019, it seems reasonable to expect that it may still be relatively low around the time of the presidential election in November 2020. But historic lows in the unemployment rate are difficult to maintain, especially following a rise in interest rates (as occurred in 2017 and 2018), which is likely to cause housing and auto sales to slow. Plus, other risks — like tariffs — also present downside risks to growth.

This means that the U.S. unemployment rate could be higher by the time of the 2020 presidential election. Based on the historical data of the past century regarding the U.S. economy and elections, this would make the probability of a Trump reelection seem less likely.

The Political Chessboard and Battleground States

As in 2020 — and most U.S. presidential elections — the geographic chessboard of electoral votes is set well ahead of the election, with battleground swing states holding critical sway over the outcome of the presidential election. I discussed this topic in Chapter 3.

But it appears as if the one thing that could potentially swing battleground states — and the election in general — is the unemployment rate, as the data in Figure 6-1 implies with regards to second-term electability. It makes sense that jobs matter. They always do! And the state of jobs and unemployment will likely matter in the 2020 election as well.

Figure 6-1: Economic Data Changes

Economic Indicators	Presidential Term of Midterm / Midterm Election Year	Truman 1950	EH 1954	EH 2 1958	JFK/LBJ 1962	LBJ 1966	Nixon 1970	Nixon/Ford 1974	Carter 1978	Regan 1982	Regan 2 1986	Bush41 1990	Clinton 1994	Clinton 2 1998	Bush 43 2002	Bush43 2 2006	Obama 2010	Obama 2 2014
Housing Starts	Midterm Election Month (Nov)				1622	961	1647	1026	2094	1372	1623	1145	1511	1660	1753	1570	545	1001
	Month Before Next Pres Election (Oct)				1524	1569	2485	1629	1523	1590	1522	1204	1392	1549	2072	777	915	1327
	Change				-98	608	838	603	-571	218	-101	99	-119	-111	319	-793	370	326
Industrial Production	Midterm Election Month (Nov)	3.4	-0.1	0.7	1.1	2.5	-2.4	-2.5	3.3	-3.3	0.9	0.1	4.4	3.2	3.1	1.6	4.8	3.8
	Month Before Next Pres Election (Oct)	1.8	0.7	0.8	1.3	2.0	4.3	3.0	-1.7	2.9	1.9	1.9	3.8	2.4	3.2	-7.4	1.8	-1.3
	Change	-1.6	0.8	0.1	0.2	-0.5	6.7	5.5	-5.0	6.2	1.0	1.8	-0.6	-0.8	0.1	-9.0	-3.0	-5.1
Unemployment Rate	Midterm Election Month (Nov)	4.2	5.3	6.2	5.7	3.6	5.9	6.6	5.9	10.8	6.9	6.2	5.6	4.4	5.9	4.5	9.8	5.8
	Month Before Next Pres Election (Oct)	3.0	3.9	6.1	5.1	3.4	5.6	7.7	7.5	7.4	5.4	7.3	5.2	3.9	5.5	6.5	7.8	4.9
	Change	-1.2	-1.4	-0.1	-0.6	-0.2	-0.3	1.1	1.6	-3.4	-1.5	1.1	-0.4	-0.5	-0.4	2.0	-2.0	-0.9
Auto Sales	Midterm Election Month (Nov)								15.5	12.0	14.8	13.1	15.9	16.1	16.5	16.7	12.3	17.2
	Month Before Next Pres Election (Oct)								11.4	14.6	15.2	13.7	15.3	17.5	17.5	10.9	14.8	18.2
	Change								-4.1	2.6	0.4	0.6	-0.6	1.4	1.0	-5.8	2.5	1.0
Real GDP	Growth Rate in Midterm Year	8.7	-0.6	-0.7	6.1	6.6	0.2	-0.5	5.6	-1.9	3.5	1.9	4.0	4.4	1.8	2.7	2.5	2.6
	Growth Rate in Next Presidential Year	4.1	2.1	2.6	5.8	4.9	5.3	5.4	-0.2	7.3	4.2	3.6	3.8	4.1	3.8	-0.3	2.2	1.5
	Change	-4.6	2.7	3.3	-0.3	-1.7	5.1	5.9	-5.8	9.2	0.7	1.6	-0.2	-0.4	2.0	-3.0	-0.3	-1.1

CHAPTER 7

THE IMPORTANCE OF EYES ON SCREENS

Hillary Clinton outspent Donald Trump significantly in the 2016 presidential election. In fact, according to data collected by *The Washington Post*, total 2016 election fundraising for Trump was just under $958 million, while Clinton's election fundraising was over 46 percent more, at over $1.4 billion.[1]

And yet, Hillary still lost.

Normally, money is the big metric people are watching for to determine who will win a presidential election. And there have been some election observers who have argued that pollsters got the election outcome wrong because people did not want to admit they were voting for Trump. This is something that has been referred to in political circles as the "shy Trumper."[2]

While that may be the case, there was probably something far more fundamental at play that impacted the outcome of the 2016 presidential election. It's what technology gurus and startups refer to as "eyes on screens."

In essence, even though Hillary spent more than Donald — a whopping 46 percent more — he was still on screen more than she was.

Essentially, he got free airtime. And that free airtime was a major contributing factor to his win.

So why did Trump get more airtime? The truth is, it seems that people wanted to see more of this celebrity running for president. They couldn't get enough of it.

So important was Donald Trump's presence on television that Leslie Moonves, the recently-ousted CEO of CBS, commented in February 2016 during a speech to the Morgan Stanley Technology, Media & Telecom Conference in San Francisco that the 2016 election "may not be good for America, but it's damn good for CBS." Moonves also noted that "the money's rolling in and this is fun."[3]

Trump himself repeatedly noted on the campaign trail how much the media was thrilled he was running, even though they were critical of him and they weren't treating him fairly. While many debate the fairness point, the thrilled media part cannot be contested.

People often forget that the media doesn't make money by telling a story; they make money by selling ads for toothpaste and toilet paper. And if you are glued to your screen, then they will sell more ads — and they can sell them at a higher price. And that is certainly something Trump helped in 2016.

To further underscore this point, Moonves noted in his speech that "I've never seen anything like this, and this is going to be a very good year for us. Sorry. It's a terrible thing to say. But, bring it on, Donald. Keep going."[4]

It can be no more clearly stated that the media was making more money on ads because Trump was running.

Just look at *Saturday Night Live*. The show is often a wellspring of political satire. Alec Baldwin's portrayal of Trump has been absolutely savage, and the show has been leveraging Trump controversies since Trump was elected. But don't forget that Trump was also brought on as a guest during his presidential run, and according to *Entertainment Weekly*, Trump brought *SNL* it's "biggest ratings in years."[5]

The potential importance of this dynamic became apparent to me during the 2016 presidential election season when I was sitting in a TV studio in Austin, Texas. I was prepared to do a remote Bloomberg interview on an important economic topic.

But the hit was abruptly canceled because Trump was getting out of a car.

He wasn't being interviewed.

He wasn't giving a speech.

He wasn't even expected to say a single word.

Look, I've done over a thousand television interviews, so it wasn't a surprise to have one canceled after being "in the chair." And when it happens, you just shrug and know you'll be back in a few days for another interview. Honestly, TV hits get canceled all the time.

Not long ago, I had a hit canceled after I was in the chair to do a remote CNN interview because an announcement had been made from Buckingham Palace that Meghan Markle had given birth.

Now, the baby I get. After all, this is the first American baby to be this close to the line of succession to the British throne, and it's something people had been hyped over.

I get that. I even told the producer people love stories about babies and that I would have done the same thing.

Plus, I've certainly had more than one TV hit canceled because a president gave a surprise address or speech. But when I had this particular Bloomberg Television interview canceled because candidate Trump was just getting out of a car, I knew that eyes on screens were in play.

I mean, this was Bloomberg. It wasn't like I was waiting to do a TV hit with a local channel in a town where Trump was visiting.

And the producer even told me that they weren't expecting Trump to say anything. "But he might wave or something," she told me.

In my 15 years of doing television interviews, I've never had a producer tell me that my hit was canceled because someone was getting out of a car — and that they might wave.

In that moment, it was crystal clear that the media — many stations and networks of which have since vilified Trump — were thrilled to have him on screen because it added excitement and it was good for the bottom line, just like Moonves said.

I mean, can you imagine in 2016 that any camera crew would have been excited to get a wave from Hillary Clinton? Do you think Bloomberg, CNN, or even the local news would have interrupted any broadcast anywhere to show her getting out of a car and going into a building, with merely the hope of a wave?

Absolutely not!

Now that's the power of celebrity. And the question going into the 2020 presidential election is, are there any Democratic candidates that can capture eyes on screens the way Trump did and to a certain degree still does?

Right now there aren't. As of the writing of this book, Beyoncé isn't running, Oprah isn't running, Clooney isn't running, and Michelle Obama isn't running.

Maybe the celebrity fanfare has worn off for Trump and he won't have the same ability to leverage free airtime with eyes on screens as the first time around. For a Democratic candidate to win in 2020, that would probably need to be true.

CHAPTER 8

THE INCUMBENT ADVANTAGE

People often talk about the fact that incumbents running for president have an advantage over nonincumbents. And they do.

It's an argument that makes sense. After all, presidents theoretically have a greater ability to get eyes on screens, and they are already traveling around the country on Air Force One. This means that they can better project their candidacy — and they can use government funds and resources to do so. Plus, incumbents typically face much less of a serious challenge in the primary season, which allows party leadership and donors to allocate their funds to the person who is likely to be the presidential candidate.

In competitive primaries, donors spend a fortune on candidates who will never be president, because they won't get their party nomination. This means that in the 2020 election season, Democrats will spend millions on 19 of the 20 candidates who will not be nominated. Meanwhile, Republicans can keep their powder dry to support Trump in the general election.

Incumbency does offer an advantage to candidates, but it has historically been less of an advantage for Republican candidates than for Democratic candidates.

Since, 1900, six Republican presidents have been elected to a second term. There were four who were not reelected: Taft, Hoover, Ford, and George H. W. Bush. Additionally, Harding died in office.[1]

In contrast to Republicans, who have a 63.6% success rate of reelection, Democrats have an 87.5% success rate of reelection. Since 1900, seven Democrats have been elected to a second term. Only Carter was not reelected. Additionally, JFK died in office.[2]

Although that's a smaller number of Democratic presidents overall, the odds of reelection have been historically much higher for Democrats. But they also favor Republican incumbents.

This means that even if Trump can't get eyes on screens as a celebrity, he is still likely to get eyes on screens as the current sitting U.S. president. It also means that his odds for reelection right out of the gate are better than even, based on historical statistics for Republican presidents.

There is one other important statistic to consider about Trump's candidacy. Like the two current leading Democratic contenders — Biden and Sanders — he is an older candidate. In fact, Trump will be 74 at the time of the 2020 election. If he wins, he will be the oldest president ever reelected. Ronald Reagan was previously the oldest president reelected at age 73.[3]

CHAPTER 9

ECONOMIC CONDITIONS AHEAD OF THE 2020 ELECTION

The current business cycle expansion is on the verge of being the longest expansion in history. Plus, the most recent unemployment rate was only 3.6 percent for May 2019, which is the lowest rate since December 1969.

Although there has been significant slowing in global growth and global manufacturing, the U.S. economy is on solid footing — for now. But a lot can change in 16 months, and any slowing of the economy can only hurt Trump as an incumbent and help his future Democratic challenger.

Different Economic Backdrops
The economic outlook ahead of the 2016 presidential election was uncertain. Business investment had been in a recession during parts of 2015 and 2016.

In mid-2016, the outlook was not good. Surveys of the clients of my firm, Prestige Economics, indicated that 2017 was most likely to be a year of recession, as you can see in Figure 9-1.

Since the 2016 presidential election, however, U.S. economic data have strengthened. The U.S. unemployment rate fell in May 2019 to 3.6 percent — the lowest level since December 1969.

Meanwhile, equity markets that had been under pressure in 2015 and 2016 surged in 2017 on a revaluation trade driven and fueled by optimism about U.S. tax reform and expectations of U.S. tax cuts.

Some market analysts had the rise in equities during 2017 all wrong. Many said it was a reflation trade, but more savvy analysts with a deeper understanding of business valuation theory saw the reduction of tax rates as a factor that could mathematically bolster companies' valuations.

Figure 9-1: Expected Timing of the Next Recession in 2016[1]

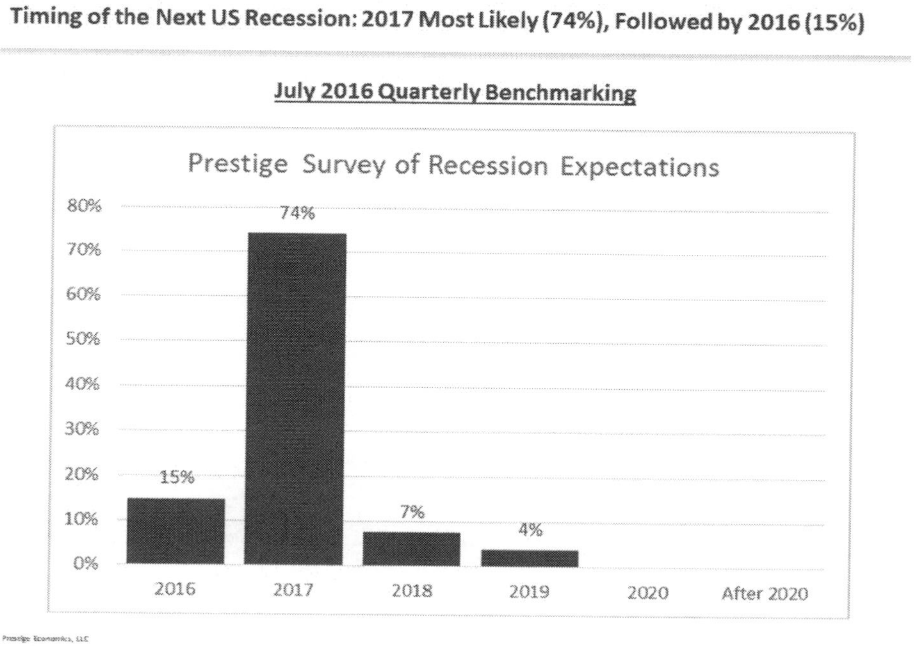

Timing of the Next US Recession: 2017 Most Likely (74%), Followed by 2016 (15%)

July 2016 Quarterly Benchmarking

Prestige Economics, LLC

A significantly positive economic impact following the outcome of the 2016 presidential election — and the expectation that company valuations could increase with lower corporate taxes — was an increase in corporate optimism. After President Trump's election, executives became more willing to invest in their businesses. This business investment supported GDP growth in 2017. It also supported equity markets.

In stark contrast to concerns about imminent recession in mid-2016, the recent survey we conducted with Prestige Economics clients in April 2019 showed that our clients believe the next recession is most likely to start in 2020. But our clients also believe that there is a zero percent chance of a recession start in 2019. These are more positive expectations than in 2016.

Figure 9-2: Expected Timing of the Next Recession in 2019[2]

<u>Q2 2019:</u> Timing of the Next US Recession Most Likely in 2020

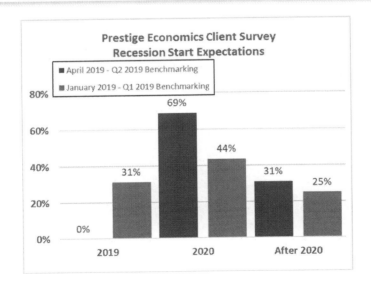

Domestic Data and Fed Policy

There are a number of different U.S. data series in this chapter to show the current level of U.S. economic growth and activity. In Chapter 12, we will look at how presidential election outcomes have historically impacted some of these data. The right place to begin an examination of the state of the economy is by looking at relevant domestic data. Thereafter, we will briefly examine some important international economic data.

Domestically, it's good to think of the most important economic data as growth, unemployment, and inflation. These data are important because they directly influence the policy of the Federal Reserve, also known as the Fed, which is the central bank of the United States. Fed policy is critical for financial markets as well as the economy.

Critical Indicators for Markets

In addition to these big three economic data series, this chapter includes an analysis of other U.S. economic data that I find to be extremely valuable. These data include industrial production, the ISM Manufacturing Index, housing starts, retail sales, and auto sales.

I pay close attention to industrial production and the ISM Manufacturing Index because these two data series are highly correlated with U.S. growth, and in some respects, these are leading economic indicators that help us see what the future may hold.

As I mentioned back in Chapter 1, causation and correlation are two different things. I have only analyzed historical economic data in the context of presidential election outcomes and what presidential terms have meant for the economy subsequently. At times, however, there are other external economic factors included in my analysis.

FRED Graphs and Recession Bars[3]

Most of the graphs in this chapter come from the Federal Reserve Economic Database (FRED). FRED graphs are free and easily accessible online at https://fred.stlouisfed.org/.

A critical beneficial attribute of FRED graphs is that they include vertical gray bars to indicate the timing of past recessions, as defined by the National Bureau of Economic Research (NBER). In Chapter 11, I will talk more about recession, the various definitions thereof, and what the 2020 presidential election could mean for the risk of recession.

Gross Domestic Product (GDP)

GDP is a measure of economic activity within the borders of a country. It has four main parts, including Consumption (C), Government Spending (G), Investment (I), and Net Exports (NX). As an economic equation, GDP looks like this:

$$GDP = C + G + I + NX$$

Nominal and Real GDP

GDP can be presented in nominal or real terms. Nominal GDP is U.S. growth presented in current dollars, but it is not usually used for growth comparisons over time because it includes inflation. Since inflation makes prices rise over time, nominal GDP growth is almost always positive. It has even been positive during every recession since 1958 except the Great Recession.

Figure 9-3: U.S. Nominal GDP (Year-Over-Year Rate)[4]

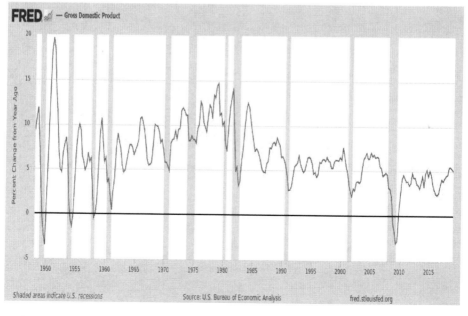

Real GDP strips out the effects of inflation and is the dominant measure of GDP that economists and professionals use to discuss economic growth. As you can see in Figure 9-4, Real GDP growth rates during the expansionary period of the current business cycle have been at consistently lower rates than in most previous business cycles.

For Q1 2019, Real GDP was +3.1 percent quarter over quarter on a seasonally adjusted annual rate. Real GDP growth has generally been modest since the Great Recession, with yearly growth rates between +1.5 percent and +2.9 percent every year since 2010. But the current business cycle began when the last recession ended, in June 2009. As of July 2019, the current business cycle will be the longest expansion in U.S. economic history.

Figure 9-4: U.S. Real GDP (Year-Over-Year Rate)[5]

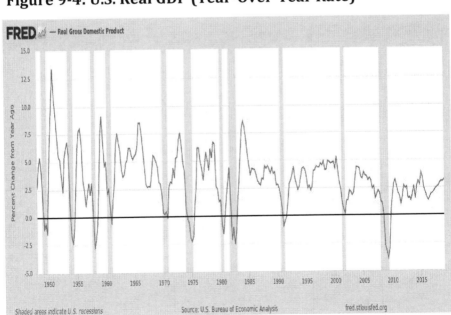

Unemployment

The unemployment rate is a critical measure of U.S. labor market health. It is also a cornerstone of one of the Fed's two dual mandates: full employment. Inflation is the second of the Fed's dual mandates.

The U.S. unemployment rate has fallen sharply since it peaked at 10.0 percent in October 2009 in the wake of the Great Recession. In May 2019, the unemployment rate in the United States was 3.6 percent. This drop has been driven by a mix of job creation and a drop in labor force participation rates. In fact, this is the lowest unemployment rate since December 1969. Needless to say, the U.S. labor market appears to be at full employment. It is also the reason wages were up 3.1 percent year on year in May 2019. This means that people have jobs — and they have money.

Figure 9-5: U.S. Unemployment Rate[6]

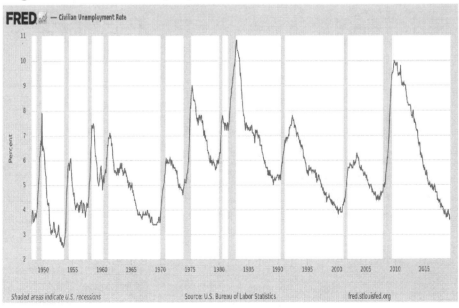

Consumer Inflation

U.S. inflation is close to the Fed's 2 percent target. Back in mid-2016, total consumer inflation, as measured by the consumer price index (CPI), was up only +0.8 percent year over year on an unadjusted basis. More recently, the CPI is well above that level — at +1.8 percent year over year in May 2019, which is just shy of the Fed's 2.0 percent inflation target. There is a second CPI series the Fed watches even more closely, called Core CPI, which excludes food and energy prices. The Core CPI was up +2.0 percent year over year in May 2019, which is just at the Fed's target. There is a very different inflation climate in 2019 compared to the low-inflation situation ahead of the 2016 presidential election. With Core CPI right at the Fed's target, it would be tough for the Fed to raise rates — and it would be tough for the Fed to cut rates.

Figure 9-6: U.S. Consumer Price Index[7]

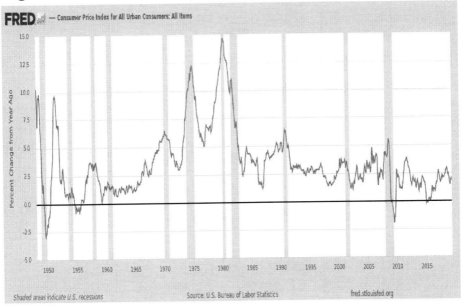

Retail Sales

Year-over-year retail sales growth is similar to modestly positive levels since in 2016. Retail sales growth was much stronger in 2017 and 2018, but it has since slowed.

The U.S. job market is on solid footing, and over 70 percent of U.S. GDP is driven by consumption. It should, therefore, not be a surprise that retail sales growth is positive even though it has slowed. People have jobs, and wages are up.

This data series will be critical to watch ahead of the 2020 presidential election. If it slows sharply, that would be indicative of weakness in the U.S. jobs market — and that could have a significant impact on President Trump's reelectability.

Figure 9-9: U.S. Retail Sales[10]

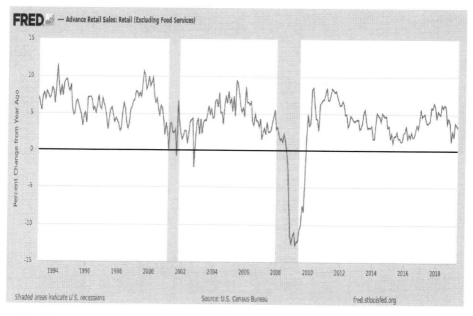

Industrial Production

Industrial production is a measure of industrial activity in factories, mining companies, and utilities. Since the Fed started collecting industrial production data in 1919, it has only been negative year over year for more than four consecutive months during recessions (or immediately after recessions). The one exception was in 2015 and 2016, when industrial production was negative year over year — but there was no recession.

Recently, U.S. industrial production has slowed sharply on a year-on-year basis. This is indicative of slowing U.S. business investment. And it supports our concerns that U.S. business investment could contract in 2019 or 2020.

Figure 9-7: U.S. Industrial Production Index[8]

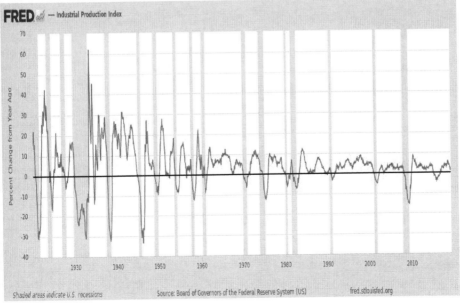

Shaded areas indicate U.S. recessions   Source: Board of Governors of the Federal Reserve System (US)   fred.stlouisfed.org

ISM Manufacturing Index

The ISM Manufacturing Index is a measure of U.S. manufacturing activity based on survey responses gathered from purchasing managers at manufacturing companies. The break-even level for this purchasing manager index is 50, and readings of the index below 50 are indicative of a month-over-month contraction in manufacturing activity. Multiple consecutive months of ISM readings below 50 are often leading indicators of a recession.

The last semirecession in U.S. manufacturing, which can be seen in the ISM Manufacturing Index, ended in February 2016. Through May 2019, there have been expansions in 38 of the previous 39 months. But the ISM Manufacturing Index has slowed sharply since October 2018. It now sits just above 50 and is indicative of a potential contraction in U.S. manufacturing.

Figure 9-8: ISM Manufacturing Index[9]

Auto Sales

Auto sales have been particularly important during the current business cycle because expansions in automotive credit were critical for growth after the Great Recession, when housing credit expansion was greatly restricted.

Auto sales were at high levels in 2016 — at 17.5 million vehicles for the year. But that rate was slower in 2017 and 2018. It was also below that level in May 2019, at 17.3 million. We had been expecting a slowing, due to rising interest rates in 2018.

While auto sales have slowed recently, total retail sales ex-autos have also slowed. In fact, the year-over-year growth in retail sales excluding autos slowed in 2019.

Figure 9-10: U.S. Auto Starts (SAAR)[11]

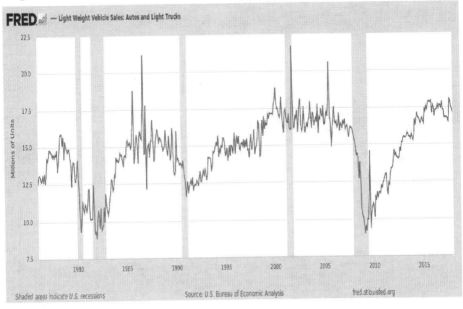

Housing Starts

Even though total U.S. housing starts have recovered since troughs seen at the end of the Great Recession, they remain low by historical standards. In fact, the current level of housing starts is still consistent with levels seen during all of the economic recessions since the 1950s — except for the 2001 recession. Housing starts remain cyclically low because they were pulled forward during the subprime boom and were subsequently depressed by restricted consumer access to housing loans.

April 2018 housing starts were at 1.287 million on a seasonally adjusted annual rate, but we cautioned that housing activity could slow as U.S. interest and mortgage rates rose in response to greater inflationary risks. Indeed, housing starts have slowed, and in April 2019, housing starts were at 1.235 million.

Figure 9-11: U.S. Housing Starts (SAAR)[12]

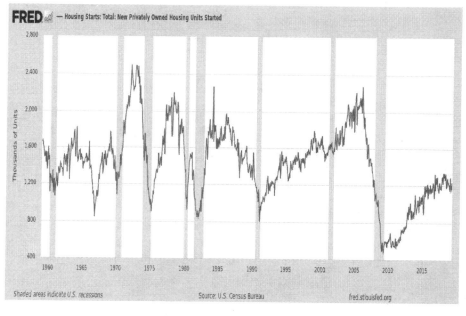

Fed Policy

Fed Funds Rates are the main policy tool of the Federal Reserve (the Fed), which is the central bank of the United States. The effective Fed Funds Rate is the interest rate at which depository institutions lend reserve balances to each other overnight.

The Fed Funds Rate is one of the main monetary policy tools that the Fed uses as a means to curb inflation — and to stimulate growth. Higher Fed Funds Rates trap liquidity and slow inflationary pressures. In the 1980s, Fed Funds Rates were used to tame high inflation, but generally low inflation rates have kept interest rates near low levels. In 2017 and 2018, inflationary pressures increased. And with rising inflation, Fed Funds Rates increased. For now, however, they are likely to remain unchanged. But there are risks of Fed cuts in 2020.

Figure 9-12: Effective Federal Funds Rate[13]

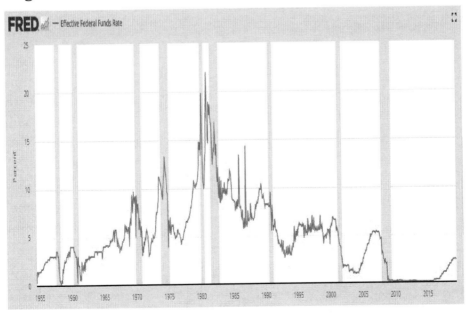

U.S. Economic Summary

U.S. economic data appear relatively solid going into the U.S. 2020 presidential election season. But the 2020 election is over 16 months away. And some industrial data has shown significant slowing.

Here is a review of some of the most critical U.S. growth data:

- **Real GDP growth** has been solid in recent quarters.
- **Nominal GDP growth** has been positive, as it usually is.
- **U.S. investment** (as a component of GDP) has been positive in recent quarters. But it could slow following higher Fed rates last year.
- **Industrial production** has been positive, but year-over-year growth rates have slowed sharply.
- **ISM Manufacturing Index** has consistently conveyed manufacturing expansions since the second half of 2016. The ISM has slowed in recent months.
- **Housing starts** have strengthened since the Great Recession, but they remain near relatively low levels that have historically only been seen during recessions.
- **Retail sales growth** has been positive, but retail sales have slowed from 2017 and 2018 levels. Autos have also slowed.
- **Inflation** is near the Fed's 2 percent target. This leaves the Fed with little wiggle room to either cut rates or raise rates.

Most U.S. economic growth data have been positive, but there has been some slowing of business investment, industrial production data, and ISM Manufacturing data. And there are further risks of slowing growth following the rise in Fed rates in 2018.

U.S. Trade Risks and Global Growth

Trade risks were extremely high last year — and they have only risen further. April 2018 IMF growth forecasts were too optimistic when they showed expectations of 3.9 percent global GDP growth for 2019. But those rates did not consider downside economic risks from tariff-related trade conflict.

The IMF subsequently lowered its global GDP growth forecasts in October 2018, January 2019, and April 2019. The IMF's 2019 global GDP growth forecast currently stands at 3.3 percent. And the IMF issued a warning about further downside risks to growth in May 2019.

The prospects of a U.S.-China trade détente are likely to remain low, as trade is not the only issue at play — despite the rhetoric. This is apparent to anyone who has read Peter Navarro's books, including *Death by China*.

In *Midterm Economics*, I warned that as the trade situation had become more critical, some manufacturing PMIs had experienced a multi-month period of slowing, underscoring potential growth risks. And there are further downside risks from current levels.

For North America, NAFTA remains a critical unresolved issue, The USMCA is a critical next step. And it could become a campaign issue in the 2020 presidential election if the USMCA is not signed by the fall of 2019.

Purchasing Manager Indices

The most important forward-looking economic indicators are purchasing manager indices (PMIs), which are surveys of purchasing managers at manufacturing firms. These are good data points for assessing growth because they are easy to understand, and they show in real time what purchasing managers — the people who buy raw materials and inputs at factories — are doing.

PMIs are easy to understand because the breakeven level for the indices is 50. In other words, if purchasing managers are buying more on a monthly basis, a PMI will be above 50, which is indicative of increased production runs for finished goods — and is a precondition for growth. Readings below 50, however, are indicative of monthly contractions. In the graphs on the following pages, the breakeven level of 50 is denoted with a solid black line.

PMIs are as close to real time as you can get for significant economic data. This is because PMIs are typically released in the first week of the month, following the month in which the data were collected.

In the United States, the ISM Manufacturing Index is a critical PMI. For international PMIs, the Chinese Caixin PMI and the Eurozone Manufacturing PMI are some of the most important.

Throughout 2018, the Eurozone Manufacturing PMI and the Chinese Caixin Manufacturing PMI slowed. They have both contracted in recent months.

Chinese Caixin Manufacturing PMI

There are two Chinese PMIs: a private PMI and a government PMI. Given questions of validity that often accompany Chinese government data, the Caixin Manufacturing PMI is one of the few consistently reliable reports since it is privately compiled.

Based on the Chinese Caixin Manufacturing PMI, the last Chinese manufacturing recession ended in June 2016. But throughout 2018, the Chinese Caixin weakened — and it has contracted in some recent months. The absolute level of the index has been lower than the ISM Manufacturing Index. Chinese Caixin PMI weakness, which can be seen in Figure 9-13, is indicative of downside risks to global growth and manufacturing. It also presents downside risks to oil prices and industrial metals prices.

Figure 9-13: Chinese Manufacturing PMI[14]

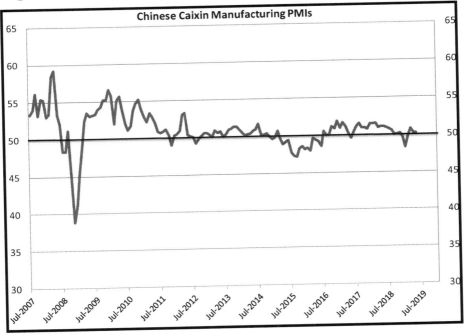

Eurozone Manufacturing PMI and Growth

Eurozone manufacturing and growth experienced a double-dip recession in the wake of the European sovereign debt crisis. As the European Central Bank reduced its balance sheet between mid-2012 and late 2014, growth in the Eurozone began to slow and the prospects of a third recession were high. With the implementation of an ECB quantitative easing program at the beginning of 2015, a third recession was averted.

The Eurozone strengthened further, with its manufacturing PMI rising to a record all-time high in December 2017. But the PMI slowed sharply in 2018 and contracted in early 2019. This underscores downside risks to Eurozone growth in 2019.

Figure 9-14: Eurozone Manufacturing PMI[15]

Global Growth Summary

Against the backdrop of higher interest rates and massive global trade risks, the outlook for global growth has weakened sharply over the past year. The International Monetary Fund (IMF) produces quarterly forecasts of global economic growth, and a 3 percent growth rate is generally accepted as the breakeven for global growth due to increases in global population. In other words, a global growth rate below 3 percent would generally be indicative of a global recession. The current IMF global GDP growth forecast for 2019 is 3.3 percent (Figure 9-15). But this rate is likely to be lowered further in July 2019. In fact, it is likely to be close to the 3 percent breakeven level. A global trade war, it turns out, has been bearish for economic growth.

Figure 9-15: IMF Growth Forecasts[16]

IMF Growth Forecasts Lowered in Oct 2018, Jan 2019, and Apr 2019

IMF Annual GDP Growth Forecasts
— April 2019 —
Real GDP, Year-over-Year % Change

	2018	2019	2020
Global	3.6	3.3	3.6
Eurozone	1.8	1.3	1.5
U.S.	2.9	2.3	1.9
Japan	0.8	1.0	0.5
U.K.	1.4	1.2	1.4
Canada	1.8	1.5	1.9
Mexico	2.0	1.6	1.9
Brazil	1.1	2.1	2.5
Russia	2.3	1.6	1.7
India	7.1	7.3	7.5
China	6.6	6.3	6.1

Source: IMF, Prestige Economics, LLC

PRESTIGE ECONOMICS

FI THE FUTURIST INSTITUTE

Economic Summary

The U.S. economy appears to be on modestly positive footing heading into the 2020 election season, but there are 16 months until the actual election. And a lot can happen to an economy in 16 months. We see the biggest downside risk to U.S. economic growth to be a further slowing of business investment and the industrial part of the economy. And tariff risks are significant.

Globally, the economic and manufacturing outlook has slowed. And there are still further downside risks to the IMF's weakened global growth forecasts. But that may be less important for the U.S. economic outlook, which is bolstered by a strong job market.

CHAPTER 10

FINANCIAL MARKETS AHEAD
OF THE 2020 ELECTION

In addition to looking at the economic backdrop ahead of the 2020 presidential election, let's examine the state of financial markets. This is an area that has been well worn for equity markets — especially for the immediate impact in the months following an election.

What I have found lacking is a longer-term analysis of the impact of election outcomes on equity markets. I have also found a lack of analysis about the impact of the outcome of U.S. presidential elections on the dollar, oil prices, silver prices, and gold prices.

This chapter tees up the analysis in Chapter 13, which looks at the impact of presidential elections on financial markets, including the Dow, the dollar, oil prices, silver prices, and gold prices. Of course, before we can perform an analysis of the impact of presidential election outcomes on financial markets, we need to look at the current state of these markets.

Dow Jones Industrial Average

The Dow Jones Industrial Average is comprised of equities from 30 of the largest public companies in the United States. These companies generally have some of the best cash positions and some of the best access to credit. The Dow usually falls during recessions, but the Dow can be resilient ahead of a recession since Dow companies often serve as a flight to quality.

The Dow experienced a surge in 2017 as equity markets reflected the potential for U.S. corporate tax cuts in a revaluation trade in Figure 10-1. The Dow remained strong until inflation risks increased in early 2018, when the Dow fell on these concerns. The Dow also came under more pressure from tariff concerns. And it has generally traded sideways over the past year and a half, although it hit record all-time highs during that period.

Figure 10-1: Dow Jones Industrial Average[1]

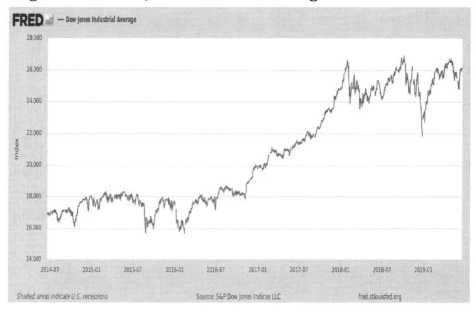

The S&P 500

The S&P 500 is comprised of 500 large equity names traded on U.S. stock exchanges. The index can be more volatile than the Dow and usually falls during a recession as well.

As with the Dow, the S&P 500 experienced a surge in 2017 as equity markets reflected the potential for U.S. corporate tax cuts in a revaluation trade. The S&P 500 remained strong until inflation risks increased in early 2018, when the S&P 500 fell on these concerns. Higher interest rates and trade risks have introduced volatility, and the S&P 500 subsequently came under pressure — especially at the end of 2018. Although it has since rebounded, it has experienced choppy trading despite a more dovish Fed because of continued tariff concerns, as seen in Figure 10-2.

Figure 10-2: S&P 500[2]

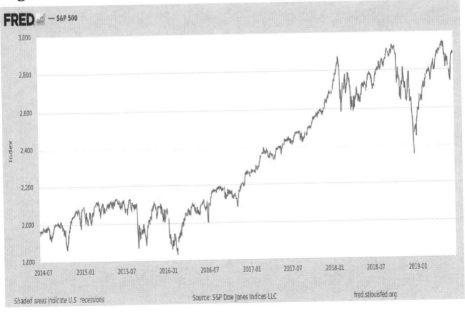

The Dollar

The dollar is represented in several different ways as a basket against major currencies, including the NYBOT dollar index (DXY) and the Bloomberg dollar (BBDXY). The Federal Reserve has its own basket, known as the trade-weighted dollar, which is used in this book for analytical purposes. The Fed's trade-weighted dollar is defined as "a weighted average of the foreign exchange value of the U.S. dollar against a subset of the broad index currencies…. Major currencies index includes the Euro Area, Canada, Japan, United Kingdom, Switzerland, Australia, and Sweden."[3] At the time this book was written, the dollar was at relatively high levels, as in Figure 10-3, but it was significantly weaker than it had been in 2016 and 2017. The dollar has generally been choppy over the past four years.

Figure 10-3: Trade-Weighted U.S. Dollar (Major Currencies)[4]

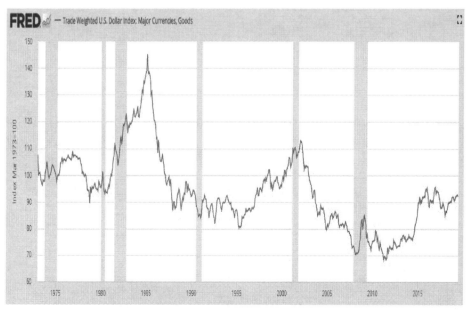

Gold Prices

Gold prices have generally trended higher since the end of Bretton Woods in the early 1970s. Gold prices spiked during the global financial crisis but subsequently fell when the dollar strengthened during the period following the European sovereign debt crisis. Gold prices remain relatively elevated, however, considering the level of the greenback, which is strong.

At the time this book was written, the price of gold had been choppy in recent years, although it has generally trended choppily higher since early 2016, but it remained sharply lower than during 2011 and 2012.

Throughout this book, I have used nominal monthly gold prices for my analysis, as in Figure 10-4.

Figure 10-4: Nominal Monthly Price of Gold[5]

Silver Prices

Like gold prices, silver prices have generally trended higher since the end of Bretton Woods in the early 1970s. Silver prices spiked during the global financial crisis but subsequently fell when the dollar strengthened during the period following the European sovereign debt crisis. Nevertheless, silver prices are relatively elevated considering the level of the greenback.

At the time this book was written, the price of silver had been under pressure from a strong dollar and a slowdown in global manufacturing. I have used nominal monthly silver prices in my analysis, as in Figure 10-5.

Figure 10-5: Nominal Monthly Price of Silver[6]

Crude Oil Prices

Crude oil prices surged ahead of the Great Recession, then collapsed, and then rebounded quickly. Advances in shale drilling technology in the United States allowed new oil supply to come quickly to market, and oil prices came under pressure with the onset of a Chinese manufacturing recession that lasted from late 2014 through mid-2016. After mid-2016, however, oil prices trended higher before coming under pressure on downside risks to global growth, global trade, and Chinese manufacturing in the latter part of 2018.

Crude oil prices have been struggling to show support at the time of this book's publication due to mixed dynamics of increasing U.S. supplies, weak global growth, strong U.S. driving demand, and a potentially tenuous coordinated effort by OPEC and non-OPEC countries to keep OPEC+ oil production at reduced levels.

Figure 10-6: Nominal Monthly Price of Crude Oil[7]

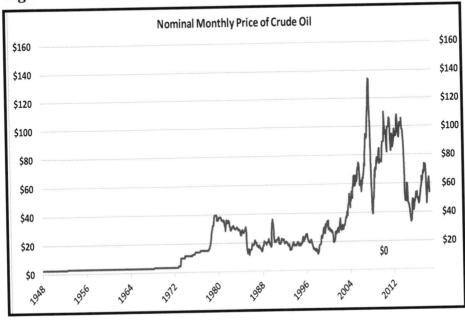

Financial Markets Summary

At the time this book was written, U.S. equity indices were near all-time highs, and the dollar was strong. But oil prices and industrial metals prices were under pressure. Industrial metals were under the most pressure on elevated risks of a global manufacturing slowdown. At the same time, silver and gold prices, which had been trending higher over multiple years, were also experiencing choppy trading due to an elevated greenback and relatively high equity markets.

In Chapter 13, I will examine the impact of presidential elections on these financial markets. Interestingly, economic data tend to be more impacted by election outcomes than financial markets. This is likely the case, because most trends in financial markets are dependent on longer-term dynamics in play, rather than specific election outcomes.

CHAPTER 11

ELECTIONS AND RECESSIONS

The United States has been in an economic expansion since mid-2009. In July 2019, just after this book comes out, the current economic expansion will be the longest in the history of the United States.

But despite this strength, the question on many people's minds is, when will the next recession start? Another recession is coming. But that's just because another recession is always coming.

Historically, presidential elections have been very closely tied to recessions. The timing of U.S. recession starts coincides so closely with U.S. presidential elections that there is a discernable level of *election cyclicality*. And historical recession starts have occurred so closely around U.S. presidential elections, in fact, that they fit within relatively tight *election-recession windows*. The mean recession start for pre-election recessions since 1928 was 9.3 months before presidential elections.

If this time isn't different, then the clock is ticking.

Before digging much further into *election cyclicality* and the *election-recession window*, it is important to look at how the definition of recession has changed — and when recessions have historically occurred.

Recession Defined

Recessions have been traditionally defined by economists as two or more consecutive quarters of negative Gross Domestic Product growth, otherwise known as GDP. During those two or more quarters, the level of GDP falls. This doesn't mean that GDP as a sum of consumption, government spending, investment, and net exports is negative; it means that the level of growth declines, which means the percent change from one quarter to the next quarter is negative.

The National Bureau of Economic Research (NBER) is a recognized authority on business cycle research in the United States, including the timing of U.S. recessions. Since 2010, the NBER has been using a slightly different definition of recession than the traditional definition involving two negative consecutive quarters of growth: "a recession is a significant decline in economic activity spread across the economy, lasting more than a few months, normally visible in Real GDP, real income, employment, industrial production, and wholesale-retail sales."[1]

The NBER defines itself as "a private, non-profit, non-partisan organization dedicated to conducting economic research and to disseminating research findings among academics, public policy makers, and business professionals," according to the NBER website at www.nber.org.[2]

The Federal Reserve Economic Database (FRED) of the St. Louis Fed uses the NBER definitions of historical recessions to determine the placement of shaded recession bars on FRED economic and financial market graphs, as seen throughout this book — especially in Chapters 9 and 14.

Since the NBER definition of recession is good enough for the Fed, it's good enough for us! This is why I have used the NBER dates and definition of recession throughout this book.

A table of NBER recession dates can be seen in Figure 11-1, which is followed by an analysis of the relationship between recession starts and presidential elections.

Pre-Election Recessions and Post-Election Recessions
For the purposes of my analysis on the following pages, a *pre-election recession* is defined as a recession that starts less than 24 months before a presidential election.

A *post-election recession* is defined as a recession that starts less than 24 months following a presidential election, including the recession of November 1948, which started during the month of a presidential election.

Since 1854, there have not been any recessions that started exactly 24 months from a presidential election. So that wasn't a problem in determining if an election should be a pre-election recession or a post-election recession.

Figure 11-1: Recession Dates According to the NBER[3]

<table>
<tr><th colspan="2" align="center">BUSINESS CYCLE
REFERENCE DATES</th></tr>
<tr><th>Peak</th><th>Trough</th></tr>
<tr><td colspan="2" align="center">Quarterly dates
are in parentheses</td></tr>
<tr><td></td><td>December 1854 (IV)</td></tr>
<tr><td>June 1857(II)</td><td>December 1858 (IV)</td></tr>
<tr><td>October 1860(III)</td><td>June 1861 (III)</td></tr>
<tr><td>April 1865(I)</td><td>December 1867 (I)</td></tr>
<tr><td>June 1869(II)</td><td>December 1870 (IV)</td></tr>
<tr><td>October 1873(III)</td><td>March 1879 (I)</td></tr>
<tr><td>March 1882(I)</td><td>May 1885 (II)</td></tr>
<tr><td>March 1887(II)</td><td>April 1888 (I)</td></tr>
<tr><td>July 1890(III)</td><td>May 1891 (II)</td></tr>
<tr><td>January 1893(I)</td><td>June 1894 (II)</td></tr>
<tr><td>December 1895(IV)</td><td>June 1897 (II)</td></tr>
<tr><td>June 1899(III)</td><td>December 1900 (IV)</td></tr>
<tr><td>September 1902(IV)</td><td>August 1904 (III)</td></tr>
<tr><td>May 1907(II)</td><td>June 1908 (II)</td></tr>
<tr><td>January 1910(I)</td><td>January 1912 (IV)</td></tr>
<tr><td>January 1913(I)</td><td>December 1914 (IV)</td></tr>
<tr><td>August 1918(III)</td><td>March 1919 (I)</td></tr>
<tr><td>January 1920(I)</td><td>July 1921 (III)</td></tr>
<tr><td>May 1923(II)</td><td>July 1924 (III)</td></tr>
<tr><td>October 1926(III)</td><td>November 1927 (IV)</td></tr>
<tr><td>August 1929(III)</td><td>March 1933 (I)</td></tr>
<tr><td>May 1937(II)</td><td>June 1938 (II)</td></tr>
<tr><td>February 1945(I)</td><td>October 1945 (IV)</td></tr>
<tr><td>November 1948(IV)</td><td>October 1949 (IV)</td></tr>
<tr><td>July 1953(II)</td><td>May 1954 (II)</td></tr>
<tr><td>August 1957(III)</td><td>April 1958 (II)</td></tr>
<tr><td>April 1960(II)</td><td>February 1961 (I)</td></tr>
<tr><td>December 1969(IV)</td><td>November 1970 (IV)</td></tr>
<tr><td>November 1973(IV)</td><td>March 1975 (I)</td></tr>
<tr><td>January 1980(I)</td><td>July 1980 (III)</td></tr>
<tr><td>July 1981(III)</td><td>November 1982 (IV)</td></tr>
<tr><td>July 1990(III)</td><td>March 1991(I)</td></tr>
<tr><td>March 2001(I)</td><td>November 2001 (IV)</td></tr>
<tr><td>December 2007 (IV)</td><td>June 2009 (II)</td></tr>
</table>

As you will see, most recessions have been post-election recessions and the *election-recession window* has narrowed over time. Although we are not in an *election-recession window* right now, we are quickly approaching one.

Important Recession Facts from the NBER
As you can see in the table in Figure 11-1, there have been 33 recessions since 1854, which is the oldest date for which the NBER has analyzed business cycles and recessions. For purposes of my analysis, I have only considered these 33 recessions when evaluating the impact of presidential elections on the business cycle and recession starts.

Recession Starts Since 1854
As I mentioned at the beginning of this chapter, we are most concerned with the timing of recession starts since the current U.S. business cycle has gone some time since the last recession started in December 2007.

Of the 33 recessions since 1854, 23 recessions (or 70 percent) started in the 24 months after the presidential election month and are post-election recessions. Meanwhile 10 recessions (or 30 percent) started before the presidential election month and are pre-election recessions. This data shows that a recession is significantly more likely to start in the 24 months after a presidential election than it is likely to start in the 24 months before.

But how long after a presidential election does a post-election recession usually start? In truth: not long at all!

Recession Starts Since 1854

Post-election recessions, which have been 70 percent of recessions since 1854, have had a median recession start only 9 months after a presidential election. The mean recession start for these post-election recessions was 10.5 months after an election.

Similarly, pre-election recessions tend to start not long before an election. Pre-election recessions, which have been 30 percent of recessions since 1854, have had a median recession start that was 11.5 months before an election. The mean recession start for these pre-election recessions was 12.4 months before an election. These starts can be seen in Figure 11-2.

Recession Starts Since the Great Depression

Some readers may take issue with the recessions that started back in the 1800s. After all, the economy is vastly different now than it was then. The economy was still predominantly agrarian in the mid-1800s, before it transitioned to a manufacturing and industrial economy and thereafter (and more recently) to a service sector economy.

You might think that recession starts would be drastically different for a more modern time period — say, since the Great Depression. But that is not the case. In fact, the likelihood of a post-election recession start has increased, while the timing of recession starts has come closer to presidential elections. Both pre-election and post-election recessions have started closer to presidential elections since 1928 than they did between 1854 and 1928.

There have been 14 recessions since 1928, beginning with the Great Depression that started in 1929 and ending with the Great Recession that started in 2007.

Since 1928, 11 of 14 recessions (79 percent) started after presidential elections. Those post-election recession starts had a median recession start that was only 8 months after a presidential election. The mean recession start for the same recessions was 8.4 months after a presidential election.

Three recessions since 1928 started before presidential elections. These pre-election recession starts had a median recession start that was 10 months before the election. The mean recession start for the same recessions was 9.3 months before the election.

A comparison of pre-election recession starts and post-election recession starts since 1854 and 1928 can be seen in Figure 11-2. As noted previously, the biggest difference is that recession starts have occurred more closely to presidential elections since 1928.

Figure 11-2: Pre-Election and Post-Election Recession Starts

	Pre-Election Recession Starts Months Before Election	Post-Election Recession Starts Months After Election
Since 1854		
Median	11.5	9.0
Mean	12.4	10.5
Since 1928		
Median	10.0	8.0
Mean	9.3	8.4

Election-Recession Window

The time periods before presidential elections and after presidential elections have been filled with recessions. Since most recessions have historically started less than a year before or after a presidential election, this period can reasonably be called the *election-recession window*.

Election-Recession Window Narrows

In addition to having a historical election-recession window, in which a recession would start during the year before or (more likely) the year after a presidential election, the mean and median start dates of recessions have occurred closer to presidential elections since 1928. Furthermore, even the outlier recession starts have become less frequent and closer to elections. As such, the election-recession window has narrowed.

For all elections since 1854, pre-election recession starts occurred between 1 and 20 months prior to presidential elections. Since 1928, however, the distribution has become tighter, with every pre-election recession starting between 7 and 11 months before a presidential election. Of course, the sample size is smaller since 1928 because there have only been three examples of pre-election recession starts. Nevertheless, the election-recession window for pre-election recessions has become much tighter. The same is true for post-election recessions.

For all elections since 1854, post-election recession starts occurred between 0 and 23 months after presidential elections. Since 1928, however, the distribution has become narrower, with every post-election recession starting between 0 and 20 months after a presidential election. Although this range does not look much tighter, the tails on the distribution of post-election recession starts are much wider before 1928.

If we go back to 1854, there have been seven post-election recessions that started more than 13 months after a presidential election, with six of them occurring prior to 1928. Since 1928, however, only one post-election recession has occurred more than 13 months after a presidential election.

Excluding the 1990 Recession

When we look at the post-election recessions since 1928, the recession of 1990 is an exception because it started much longer after a presidential election (20 months after). If we exclude the 1990 recession, 10 of the 11 post-election recession starts since 1928 occurred between 0 and 13 months after a presidential election. That's 91 percent.

If we look at all post-election recessions back to 1854, that percentage was a much lower 70 percent. And for post-election recession starts between 1854 and 1928, only 50 percent started in the 13 months following a presidential election. Post-election recessions between 1854 and 1928 were just as likely to start more than 13 months following a presidential election.

Election-Recession Window Minimums and Maximums

The width of the election-recession window is determined by the maximum and minimum number of months recession starts have occurred historically in temporal proximity to presidential elections. As I mentioned in the previous section, since 1854, the maximum number of months for a pre-election recession start was 20 months before a presidential election. During that same time period, the maximum number of months for a post-election recession start was 23 months after a presidential election.

Since 1928, however, the election-recession window has narrowed. The maximum number of months for a pre-election recession start was 11 months before a presidential election. During that same time period, the maximum number of months for a post-election recession start (excluding 1990) was 13 months after a presidential election. If we include 1990, the maximum time for a post-election recession start was 20 months after a presidential election. The maximum and minimum number of months recession starts have occurred from presidential elections can be seen in Figure 11-3.

Figure 11-3: Recession Start Month Minimums and Maximums

	Pre-Election Recession Starts Months Before Election	Post-Election Recession Starts Months After Election
Since 1854		
Mininum	1	0
Maximum	20	23
Since 1928		
Minimum	7	0
Maximum	11	20
Max (ex 1990)		13

Election Cyclicality

The coincidence of elections with business cycles is something I call *election cyclicality*, which occurs independently of the president's political party. It has two main parts: the election-recession window and the term limit on growth. As I mentioned in a previous chapter, correlation does not equal causation. Nevertheless, there is a high correlation between the timing of recession starts and elections.

Term Limit on Growth

Since the National Bureau of Economic Research's earliest data on U.S. business cycles in 1854, the maximum number of full presidential terms without the start of a new recession has been two. There have never been three consecutive full presidential terms without a recession start. In this case, a full presidential term is defined as the four-year period between elections during which one or more individuals may have been president.

Since the last U.S. recession was the Great Recession (starting before President Obama's first term), the conclusion of Obama's second term without a recession start puts us at the historical maximum of two presidential terms without the start of a recession. Two terms without a recession start is the *term limit on growth*. Based on historical data, the next recession start seems likely in 2019 or 2020.

Economic Impact Summary

The United States has been in an expansion for almost a decade — since the end of the Great Recession in mid-2009. This makes the timing of the next recession start critical. The two attributes of election cyclicality and term limits on growth point to the likelihood of a coming recession.

Our analysis of NBER historical data for recessions since 1854 indicates that a recession is likely to start before the end of Trump's current presidential term. But it could actually be different this time, given the current strength of the U.S. labor market, even though the term limit on growth points to the high likelihood of a recession before the end of the current presidential term in 2020.

Although political party affiliation is unimportant for election cyclicality, the election-recession window, and the term limit on growth, it is very important for the unemployment rate and industrial production.

CHAPTER 12

ECONOMIC IMPACTS

As you may have noticed, I have not mentioned the party affiliation of presidents so far when looking at past economic dynamics and recessions. This is because *election cyclicality* occurs independently of the president's party. This is not true of other economic data, however. In this chapter, I will examine the impact of presidential elections and the party affiliation of winning candidates on economic data other than GDP growth, including unemployment, industrial production, housing starts, and auto sales.

Tenure of Presidency
My analysis in this chapter of economic data is based on evaluating changes that occurred during what I call the *tenure of presidency* or *presidential tenure*. This is the time frame in the postwar period during which an elected president took office (January) until the last full month of his tenure (December), whether that was at the end of a single term — or at the end of two terms.

Shared Presidential Tenure

I controlled for the shared postwar presidential tenures of JFK and LBJ, as well as Nixon and Ford, by grouping them together. I grouped JFK and LBJ into one administration since LBJ became president in the first half of JFK's term. I grouped Nixon with Ford into one administration because Ford became president during Nixon's second term and Ford was never elected president.

Controlling for the Impact of Previous Presidential Tenure

In my analysis, it was also important to control for the impact of a previous presidential tenure on the state of the economy when a new president was elected. In order to achieve this end, I compared the best and worst figures for economic indicators during the first year of a new presidential tenure with the figures at the end of that presidential tenure, whether it was an individual or shared term.

In comparing how unemployment, industrial production, housing starts, and auto sales changed at the end of a presidential tenure (shared or not), it seemed valuable to compare ending levels to the best and worst levels seen in the first year because those levels could have been reasonably blamed on — or credited to — a predecessor. Improvements from the worst levels in the first year to the end of a president's term or tenure could reasonably be credited to that president. Similarly, a significant worsening of economic conditions from the best levels in the first year to the end of a new president's term or tenure could also be reasonably attributed to that president.

In my analysis of the impact of presidential elections on financial markets in Chapter 13, a more immediate impact was assumed, given the more rapid response of financial markets compared to the economy.

Now let's take a look at unemployment, industrial production, housing starts, and auto sales.

Unemployment

The unemployment rate is one of the most critical U.S. economic indicators, and its changes have been highly correlated with the political party of the president since 1948. In fact, since Truman's election in 1948, the unemployment rate has risen during every Republican presidential tenure except for Reagan. Conversely, the unemployment rate has fallen during every Democratic presidential tenure since Truman's election in 1948 except for Carter, when the impact was mixed.

The changes in the U.S. unemployment rate from the lowest and highest rates of the first year until the end of a presidential tenure can be seen in Figure 12-1.

Decreases in the unemployment rate are in green as well as underlined and bolded. Increases in the unemployment rate are in red, and Carter's mixed changes have been left unshaded and unbolded in the table.

A starker presentation of the change in the unemployment rate during a presidential tenure can be seen more clearly when we compare the percentage point changes from the highest and lowest levels seen in the first year of a presidential tenure (Year 1) with the ending level of unemployment of that presidential tenure. This is seen in the left two columns of Figure 12-1. These columns show the differences in the unemployment rate in percentage points. Since a lower unemployment rate is more positive, negative changes are the most positive for the labor market. I have bolded, underlined, and shaded in green the biggest declines in the unemployment rate in percentage points.

The right two columns in Figure 12-2 show how large a percent change the increase or decrease in the unemployment rate was from the lowest and highest rates in the first year of a presidential tenure (Year 1) to the end of the presidential tenure. I have bolded, underlined, and shaded in green the most positive percent changes in the unemployment rate.

Correlation does not mean causation, but there is an extremely high correlation between changes in the unemployment rate and the party affiliation of a presidential tenure.

There could be any number of reasons why the unemployment rate has usually declined during Democratic presidential tenures but has usually risen during Republican presidential tenures. This could be, for example, the result of fiscal policies designed to stimulate employment, or it could be affected by a Democratic party focus on workers.

Figure 12-1: Unemployment and Presidential Tenure[1]

President	Party	Lowest Unemployment Rate in Year 1	Highest Unemployment Rate in Year 1	Ending Unemployment Rate
Truman	D	4.3%	7.9%	**2.7%**
Eisenhower	R	2.5%	4.5%	6.6%
JFK/LBJ	D	6.0%	7.1%	**3.4%**
Nixon/Ford	R	3.4%	3.7%	7.8%
Carter	D	6.4%	7.6%	7.2%
Reagan	R	7.2%	8.5%	**5.3%**
Bush 41	R	5.0%	5.4%	7.4%
Clinton	D	6.5%	7.3%	**3.9%**
Bush 43	R	4.2%	5.7%	7.3%
Obama	D	7.8%	10.0%	**4.7%**

Figure 12-2: Changes in Unemployment Rates[2]

President	Party	Percentage Point Change from Lowest in Year 1	Percentage Point Change from Highest in Year 1	Percent Change from Lowest in Year 1	Percent Change from Highest in Year 1
Truman	D	**-1.6%**	**-5.2%**	**-37%**	**-66%**
Eisenhower	R	4.1%	2.1%	164%	47%
JFK/LBJ	D	**-2.6%**	**-3.7%**	**-43%**	**-52%**
Nixon/Ford	R	4.4%	4.1%	129%	111%
Carter	D	0.8%	**-0.4%**	13%	**-5%**
Reagan	R	**-1.9%**	**-3.2%**	**-26%**	**-38%**
Bush 41	R	2.4%	2.0%	48%	37%
Clinton	D	**-2.6%**	**-3.4%**	**-40%**	**-47%**
Bush 43	R	3.1%	1.6%	74%	28%
Obama	D	**-3.1%**	**-5.3%**	**-40%**	**-53%**

It could also be, in the case of Obama, tied to the decline in labor force participation or an increase in the level of total government debt, which increased significantly during his tenure.

Regardless of the causes behind the correlations between political party and changes in the unemployment rate, it seems likely that, based on this historical data, one could reasonably expect a lower unemployment rate at the end of a tenure of a Democrat than at the end of a tenure of a Republican. Of course, past performance is not indicative of future returns. But historical data support this thesis.

Based on a long-term, secular decline in labor force participation rates, which pushes the unemployment rate lower, I have been generally expecting lower unemployment rates over time. Of course, this is not necessarily a positive way to see the unemployment rate decline: job creation is better than a shrinking labor force. But increases in automation could exacerbate declines in labor force participation. This is a subject I discuss in Chapter 14.

Industrial Production
U.S. industrial production has been higher at the end of every presidential tenure since the Second World War except for that of George W. Bush. Plus, by some measures, industrial production ended higher even at the end of George W. Bush's tenure. At the end of his second term, industrial production ended 2 percent lower than the best rate in the first year of his presidential tenure, but it also ended 3 percent higher than at the lowest level in the first year of his presidential tenure.

The implication here is that no matter who is president, industrial production is highly likely to be higher at the end of their presidential tenure.

In Figure 12-3, I have bolded and underlined the three greatest percentage increases of industrial production during presidential tenures. These all occurred under Democrats: Truman, JFK/LBJ, Clinton.

Industrial Production has so far risen under Trump as well. In fact, despite a recent slowing in the pace of manufacturing activity and industrial production, industrial production was 6.7 percent higher in May 2019 than it was in the lowest level of 2017 (President Trump's Year 1). Of course, there are some significant downside risks to the industrial part of the economy over the next 16 months, due to the past rise in interest rates in 2017 and 2018 as well as persistent trade risks.

Figure 12-3: Industrial Production Changes[3]

President	Party	Highest Industrial Production Year 1	Lowest Industrial Production in Year 1	Ending Industrial Production	Point Change from Highest in Year 1	Point Change from Lowest in Year 1	Percent Change from Highest in Year 1	Percent Change from Lowest in Year 1
Truman	D	14.6	13.6	19.7	5.1	6.1	**35%**	**45%**
Eisenhower	R	20.4	18.7	22.8	2.4	4.0	12%	21%
JFK/LBJ	D	25.6	22.8	39.1	13.5	16.3	**53%**	**72%**
Nixon/Ford	R	40.3	39.3	47.1	6.8	7.7	17%	20%
Carter	D	49.9	46.8	52.8	2.9	5.9	6%	13%
Reagan	R	53.2	51.3	63.8	10.6	12.5	20%	24%
Bush 41	R	64.0	62.9	66.3	2.3	3.3	4%	5%
Clinton	D	68.5	66.6	95.2	26.7	28.6	**39%**	**43%**
Bush 43	R	94.5	90.5	93.3	-1.3	2.8	-1%	3%
Obama	D	91.0	87.1	102.9	11.9	15.9	13%	18%

Housing Starts

There is a relatively short amount of historical housing starts data available for analysis, since it only goes back to 1959. Nevertheless, changes in housing starts have been less correlated with the party of a president than other economic indicators.

Carter, Bush 41, and Bush 43 saw the biggest drops in housing starts from the lowest levels of the first year of their presidential tenures to the end of their tenures. Obama saw the biggest increases, although that was due to the depressed level of starts at the start of his tenure during the Great Recession. Housing starts generally seem to be influenced significantly by a base effect of starts in place at the beginning of a presidential tenure.

After all, housing starts improved massively during Obama's tenure, but that was largely a function of Obama walking into office during a massive housing crisis, with very low home starts. Although starts have recovered since, they still remain near low levels that are typically consistent with recessions.

Figure 12-4: Housing Starts Changes[4]

President	Party	Highest Housing Starts Year 1	Lowest Housing Starts in Year 1	Ending Housing Starts	Change from Highest in Year 1	Change from Lowest in Year 1	Percent Change from Highest in Year 1	Percent Change from Lowest in Year 1
JFK/LBJ	D	1429	1166	1548	119	382	8%	33%
Nixon/Ford	R	1769	1229	1804	35	575	2%	47%
Carter	D	2142	1527	1482	-660	-45	-31%	-3%
Reagan	R	1547	837	1563	16	726	1%	87%
Bush 41	R	1621	1251	1227	-394	-24	-24%	-2%
Clinton	D	1533	1083	1532	-1	449	0%	41%
Bush 43	R	1670	1540	560	-1110	-980	-66%	-64%
Obama	D	594	478	1287	693	809	117%	169%

Auto Sales

Changes in lightweight vehicle sales (i.e., auto sales) seem to be relatively uncorrelated with the party of the president in office, but the changes in sales seem to be correlated with a change in presidential tenure. In keeping with a relatively short time series of auto sales data, I was expecting the current presidential tenure (regardless of party) would likely end with a significantly lower level of total light vehicle sales compared to the level at the end of President Obama's presidential tenure. After all, growth and contractions in auto sales tend to alternate (up, down, up down, etc.).

Plus, under President Obama, auto sales hit a new all-time record high for the rise in auto sales from the lowest level in Year 1 to the end of his tenure. Auto sales under President Trump were close to flat in May 2019 compared to when he took office, at a seasonally adjusted annual rate of 17.3 million vehicles, but they were up over 5 percent from the lowest level of sales in 2017 (Trump's Year 1). Much of the rise in auto sales during Obama's tenure can be attributed to low interest rates and a massive expansion of subprime auto loans. Conversely, the flat level of sales so far under Trump can be attributed to higher interest rates.

Figure 12-5: Auto Sales Changes[5]

President	Party	Highest Auto Sales Year 1	Lowest Auto Sales in Year 1	Ending Auto Sales	Change from Highest in Year 1	Change from Lowest in Year 1	Percent Change from Highest in Year 1	Percent Change from Lowest in Year 1
Carter	D	14.8	14.0	10.7	-4.1	-3.3	-28%	-24%
Reagan	R	12.5	8.8	16.1	3.6	7.2	29%	82%
Bush 41	R	16.2	13.1	13.5	-2.7	0.4	-17%	3%
Clinton	D	14.7	12.7	15.8	1.2	3.1	8%	25%
Bush 43	R	21.7	16.0	10.1	-11.6	-5.9	-53%	-37%
Obama	D	14.6	9.0	17.9	3.3	8.8	23%	98%

Fed Funds Rates and Consumer Inflation

There is a bit of an issue when looking at consumer inflation and the Fed Funds Rate because they influence each other. This can confound an analysis of the two as there can be a circular feedback loop.

One thing is clear: the biggest drivers of the Fed Funds Rate and inflation levels have not been presidential elections or the parties of presidential tenures. The biggest driver, and the most likely critical factor for the Fed Funds Rate and consumer inflation, is the proximity to the present.

Generally speaking, inflation has been pushed lower as a matter of policy since the 1980s under Fed Chairman Volcker. With relatively low levels of inflation, low levels of Fed Funds Rates have also been warranted. Although the Fed has massively expanded its balance sheet as a result of three quantitative easing programs, inflation remains relatively low.

If the past were to provide insights for the future, I would expect inflation to remain relatively low throughout the balance of President Trump's tenure — and beyond. A rise in inflation would represent a significant break in a trend that has been in place since the 1980s, and it would present significant upside risks to commodity and real estate prices while presenting downside risks to bond prices. Furthermore, U.S. inflation has struggled to remain near 2 percent, despite a massive expansion in the Fed's balance sheet. This indicates that inflation could remain stubbornly low in the near-term, especially if growth slows further.

International Economic Implications

International economic dynamics are unlikely to be influenced by the outcome of the U.S. presidential election. No matter who wins the 2020 U.S. presidential election, the risk of continued weak Chinese manufacturing is likely to remain in play. Additionally, the existential risks to the European Union and the European Monetary Union from the U.K. Brexit vote are likely to remain unaffected by the outcome of the U.S. presidential election. Plus, due to a tepid pace of global growth, downside risks to oil-based and commodity-based economies are likely to remain elevated.

Economic Impact Summary

The United States has been in an expansion for 10 years — since the end of the Great Recession in June 2019. The timing of the next recession start is critical, and the two attributes of *election cyclicality* point to the likelihood of an imminent recession.

The last recession started two presidential terms ago, and our analysis of NBER historical data for recessions since 1854 indicates that a recession is likely to start before the end of Trump's current term. This is the *term limit on growth*.

While the *term limit on growth* points to the high likelihood of a recession before the end of the next presidential term in 2020, the narrow *election-recession window*, which has been in place since 1928, points to a high probability of the next recession start occurring before the end of 2021.

While political party affiliation is unimportant for *election cyclicality*, the *election-recession window*, and the *term limit on growth*, it is very important for the unemployment rate and industrial production.

Based on historical data, it seems reasonable to expect a higher ending unemployment rate under a Republican presidential tenure and a lower ending unemployment rate under a Democratic presidential tenure. Of course, the choice now for voters isn't the same as in 2016. Voters aren't looking at new tenures for both party candidates. The choice will be to continue the current Republican tenure or to start a new Democratic tenure.

CHAPTER 13

FINANCIAL MARKET IMPACTS

We saw in the previous chapter that the outcome of presidential elections, including the party of presidential tenure, can have a significant impact on some economic indicators. In my analysis of financial markets, however, I found a different set of relationships — and almost no correlation between financial market activity and changes in the party of the president.

While my economic analysis looked at the best and worst levels of economic indicators during the first year of a presidential tenure and compared them to the ending level of that tenure, my financial market analysis compares the changes in financial markets between the month after the presidential election in December and the November of the next presidential election — as well as the November at the end of the presidential tenure period.

I structured my analysis to look for more immediate impacts of a presidential election on financial markets because financial markets respond more quickly than the economy.

The Dow Jones Industrial Average

A historical analysis of the Dow shows that the Dow ended higher during 16 of the past 22 presidential terms, if we compare the December level of the Dow in the month after a presidential election with the November of the next presidential election. This can be seen clearly in Figure 13-1. There have been only six times since 1928 that the Dow ended lower.

Implications

Generally, the Dow has risen between presidential elections, with the Dow rising in 73 percent of the presidential terms between presidential elections since 1928. It fell only 27 percent of the time between presidential elections.

Additionally, only three presidents since 1928 have seen the Dow be lower following the election of their successor (at the end of their tenure) than following their own election to the presidency. These presidents were Herbert Hoover, Jimmy Carter, and George W. Bush, who were presidents during the start of the Great Depression, the oil crisis, and the start of the Great Recession, respectively.

Past performance is not indicative of future returns, but the statistical probabilities were indicative of a stronger Dow by the November 2020 presidential election compared to the level in the month following the 2016 election (December 2016). So far in Trump's term, equity prices have risen. In fact, they rose sharply on expected corporate tax cuts during 2017. This means that equities do seem poised to end the current presidential term higher, which would be consistent with historical norms.

Figure 13-1: Percent Change in the Dow During Presidential Terms Since 1928[1]

President	Party	Dow Percent Change from December after Presidential Election Until November of Next Presidential Election
Hoover	R	-81%
FDR	D	204%
FDR	D	-28%
FDR	D	12%
FDR/Truman	D	13%
Truman	D	60%
Eisenhower	R	62%
Eisenhower	R	20%
JFK/LBJ	D	42%
LBJ	D	13%
Nixon	R	8%
Nixon/Ford	R	-7%
Carter	D	-1%
Reagan	R	23%
Reagan	R	75%
Bush 41	R	52%
Clinton	D	98%
Clinton	D	62%
Bush 43	R	-3%
Bush 43	R	-18%
Obama	D	48%
Obama	D	46%

The Dollar

Unlike other financial instruments, there did not seem to be a predictive pattern for the dollar that was influenced by the political party of the presidential candidate. Plus, U.S. presidential elections, in general, did not have a meaningful predictive impact on the direction of the dollar.

As a Chartered Market Technician looking at a chart of the U.S. trade-weighted dollar in Figure 13-2, I would note that the dollar has been trending lower since February 1985. There has been an unbroken pattern of lower highs and lower lows, which is a generally bearish price formation. As such, I would expect the dollar to fall on trend from a purely technical standpoint. It also happens to be my current forecast, based on my fundamental expectations around debt and entitlements in Chapter 14.

Figure 13-2: Trade-Weighted U.S. Dollar (Major Currencies)[2]

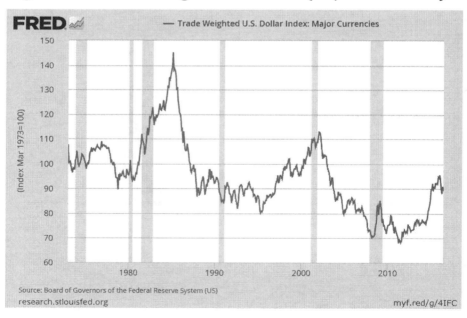

Gold Prices

There have only been four times since the end of Bretton Woods when gold prices fell from the December immediately after a president was elected until the next presidential election: Reagan's first term, George H. W. Bush's term, Clinton's second term, and Obama's second term. This means that the price of gold rose in 7 of the last 11 presidential terms, or 64 percent of the time. And gold prices have risen so far under Trump. This track record favored our expectation that gold prices would rise under on trend in the current presidential term. And we expect they will rise on trend through the next presidential term. Obviously, given the rising level of U.S. debt and entitlement exposures, there are also fundamental reasons to expect higher gold prices over time.

Figure 13-3: Percent Change in the Price of Gold During Presidential Terms Since Bretton Woods Ended[3]

President	Party	Gold Price Percent Change from December after Presidential Election Until November at end of Presidential Term
Nixon/Ford	R	104%
Carter	D	365%
Reagan	R	-43%
Reagan	R	32%
Bush 41	R	-20%
Clinton	D	13%
Clinton	D	-28%
Bush 43	R	62%
Bush 43	R	84%
Obama	D	98%
Obama	D	-29%

Silver

There have been five presidential terms since the end of Bretton Woods when silver prices fell from the December immediately after a president was elected, until the next presidential election: Reagan's first and second terms, George H. W. Bush (Bush 41)'s term, Clinton's second term, and Obama's second term. This means that the price of silver rose in 6 of the last 11 presidential terms, or about 55 percent of the time. These are less bullish dynamics than for gold prices. However, historical silver data are more bullish than this may appear since there have only been three presidents since 1928 to see lower silver prices at the end of their tenures: Reagan, George H. W. Bush, and Hoover. This historical pattern presented modest upside risks for silver prices through the current presidential term and tenure.

Figure 13-4: Percent Change in the Price of Silver During Presidential Terms Since Bretton Woods Ended[4]

President	Party	Silver Price Percent Change from December after Presidential Election Until November at end of Presidential Term
Nixon/Ford	R	111%
Carter	D	322%
Reagan	R	-55%
Reagan	R	-3%
Bush 41	R	-38%
Clinton	D	29%
Clinton	D	-4%
Bush 43	R	69%
Bush 43	R	48%
Obama	D	213%
Obama	D	-46%

Oil Prices

Since Eisenhower, from the time a president was elected until the next election at the end of his term, oil prices have ended higher 75 percent of the time. This can be seen in Figure 13-5. Oil prices have only fallen in four of 16 terms: the first term of JFK/LBJ, in both of Reagan's terms, and in Obama's second term. The declines during Reagan's terms can be attributed to the end of the oil crisis.

Figure 13-5: Percent Change in the Price of Crude Oil During Presidential Terms Since Eisenhower[5]

President	Party	Crude Oil Price Percent Change from December after Presidential Election Until November at end of Presidential Term
Eisenhower	R	10%
Eisenhower	R	5%
JFK/LBJ	D	-2%
LBJ	D	5%
Nixon	R	16%
Nixon/Ford	R	290%
Carter	D	159%
Reagan	R	-24%
Reagan	R	-45%
Bush 41	R	25%
Clinton	D	22%
Clinton	D	35%
Bush 43	R	70%
Bush 43	R	33%
Obama	D	115%
Obama	D	-46%

If we look at presidential tenure in Figure 13–6, we see that since Eisenhower, Reagan is the only president to see oil prices drop during his entire tenure as president from the month after his election until the next president was elected. I discussed this trend in *Electing Recession*, noting that this had bullish price implications for crude oil prices. Based on the historical trend of presidential cycles and oil prices, there appeared to be upside risks for oil prices during the current presidential tenure.

Of course, the low level of oil prices at the time of the 2016 presidential election, as well as the depressed level of oil and gas investment, are also factors that I noted were fundamentally likely to bolster oil prices during the current president's tenure. In the long run, I expect oil prices will rise on trend due to global demand fundamentals, like rising global population and wealth.

Figure 13-6: Percent Change in the Price of Crude Oil During Presidential Tenures Since Eisenhower[6]

President	Party	Crude Oil Price Percent Change from December after Presidential Election Until November at end of Presidential Tenure
Eisenhower	R	16%
JFK/LBJ	D	10%
Nixon/Ford	R	353%
Carter	D	159%
Reagan	R	-62%
Bush 41	R	25%
Clinton	D	77%
Bush 43	R	102%
Obama	D	21%

Summary

I have taken a presidential term and presidential tenure view of the dynamics around how presidential elections affect financial markets. This means that my expectations are predicated on the changes that occur during four-year to eight-year periods after a presidential election. Most financial markets appear to behave independently of the political party of presidential tenures, and markets tend to be driven more by secular trends, rather than by who sits in the White House.

The Dow

There have been a mere handful of cases when equity markets ended a presidential term or presidential tenure lower. Based on the historical tendency for equities to rise during most presidential tenures and terms, I wrote in *Electing Recession* that it appeared likely that the Dow would be higher at the time of the November 2020 presidential election, compared to its level in December 2016. As we look ahead to 2024, the long-term trend of a rise in equity prices over time seems likely to continue.

Dollar

Neither the party of presidential candidates nor presidential elections in general have a statistically significant impact on the dollar, based on my analysis. From a technical standpoint, there is a long-term pattern of lower highs and lower lows that has been in place for the greenback since it spiked in 1985. I expect the dollar decline to continue on trend due to fundamental risks from the rising U.S. national debt and entitlement obligations.

Oil Prices

Oil prices have trended higher for all presidents during their presidential tenures except for Ronald Reagan. Plus, in 75 percent of all presidential terms since Eisenhower, oil prices ended higher. This presented evidence of upside price risks for the current president's tenure. Longer-run fundamentals are also bullish for oil prices due to significant underinvestment and rising global oil demand growth, rising global population, and rising global wealth. These are topics I covered at length in my book *The Future of Energy*, which was released in May 2019.

Gold and Silver Prices

Gold prices have risen in 7 of the last 11 presidential terms, while silver prices have risen in 6 of the last 11 presidential terms. I noted in *Electing Recession* that this presented evidence of upside price risks for both metals through the current presidential term. There are also fundamental reasons to expect precious metals prices will rise over time, including U.S. debt and entitlement risks, which are a central topic of discussion in the next chapter.

CHAPTER 14

LONG-TERM RISKS
UNLIKELY TO CHANGE

While there is often a focus on how financial markets and the economy could be impacted by individual elections, the most important factors are unlikely to change. In part, this is because of systemic developments that have persisted through countless permutations of political party victories. The national debt, entitlements, and demographic challenges loom large over the future of the American economy, but they go largely ignored. This also means that the candidates in the current election cycle are unlikely to tackle these truly massive challenges. In fact, the Republican Party, which has branded itself as the party of fiscal conservatives, appeared to abandon its fiscal conservatism to pass the 2017 tax cuts as well as in subsequent spending bills.

Meanwhile, trade policy and Fed policy — both of which threaten U.S. growth and financial markets in the near term — were not impacted by the outcome of the U.S. midterm elections, which is something I warned about. After all, the president retained his unilateral powers to make tariff policies.

Trade Policy

In *Midterm Economics*, I noted that the president has almost unlimited unilateral authority to issue tariffs without consulting the legislative branch of government. This means that no matter what happened to the seat count in the House or the Senate for Democrats in the 2018 midterms, the president would still have this power. For this reason, I warned that tariffs were likely to play a central part in a geopolitical *opéra bouffe* at least until 2020 — and very likely beyond. As I expected, the situation with China has been made worse. And while a change of party could have a big impact on the U.S. approach to using tariffs as a diplomatic tool, some of the conflict with China is unlikely to go away. The economic conflict between the two countries may be difficult to walk back completely — if either party even wants to.

Fed Policy

Fed policy operates independently of the executive, legislative, and judicial branches of government, and the Fed was on a planned hawkish course until a slowing of some recent economic data changed the Fed's tune from hawkish to dovish. As I warned in *Midterm Economics*, if the U.S. economy slows, the Fed would likely cut policy rates — and the Fed is highly likely to engage in additional quantitative easing and balance sheet expansion in the future. This policy worked to stimulate the U.S. economy, and I expect the Fed will do it again. Furthermore, Janet Yellen noted at Jackson Hole in 2016 that "I expect that forward guidance and asset purchases will remain important components of the Fed's policy toolkit," noting also that "Future policymakers may wish to explore the possibility of purchasing a broader range of assets."[1]

In other words, the Fed is not just likely to engage in quantitative easing again in the future, but the Fed is likely to buy different kinds of securities as well. For now, however, the Fed is likely to be on hold, although a cut looks like the most likely next move.

Economic Cycle in Context
The unemployment rate is near historically low levels, the Fed is raising rates, and trade policy presents significant risks to corporate profits. These factors are coming together at a time when the U.S. economy has had one of the longest expansionary runs in U.S. history.

In light of our current point in the business cycle, these risks indicate that the end of the cycle is coming. Although a recession does not appear to be imminent — something that is also underscored by my analysis of historical election cyclicality data — the current cycle will come to an end. And most of the cycle is very likely behind us.

Long-Term Risks
Against the backdrop of near-term political and economic policy dynamics that seem unlikely to change, there are four other major risk factors that are unlikely to change but that pose significant medium-term and long-term risks to the U.S. economy.

These are the four major long-term risks:
   1) U.S. National Debt
   2) Entitlements
   3) Demographics
   4) Automation

The National Debt

The U.S. national debt is a growing problem. At almost $22 trillion, the national debt is not a small sum. In fact, it comes out to almost $68,024 for every man, woman, and child living in the United States of America.[2]

That is a lot of debt!

As you can see in Figure 14-1, the pace at which the U.S. national debt is rising has accelerated. It took 205 years for the U.S. national debt to exceed $1 trillion, which happened in October 1981. But it then took less than five years for the national debt to double to $2 trillion in April 1986. The most recent doubling of the U.S. national debt occurred during the current business cycle — in the wake of the Great Recession.[3]

Although not as pronounced as the trend in total U.S. government debt, the debt-to-GDP ratio has risen sharply since the onset of the Great Recession as well (Figure 14-2). One major negative impact of a high national debt is the drag on potential future U.S. economic growth as measured by Gross Domestic Product — or GDP. Plus, debt exposures can be exacerbated by compounding interest on already outstanding government debt.

Although some analysts are quick to note that our debt-to-GDP ratio is lower than other countries, it is also important to note that the U.S. economy is the largest in the world. This means that rising U.S. debt levels could make it more difficult for the global economy to absorb U.S. debt issuances over time.

Figure 14-1: Total U.S. Federal Debt[4]

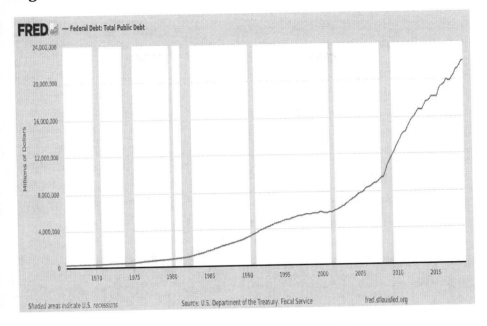

Figure 14-2: Total Federal Debt as a Percent of GDP[5]

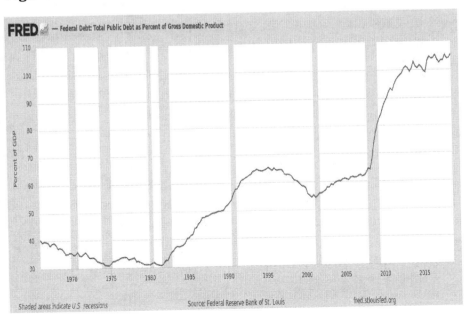

But despite the rising U.S. national debt — both in absolute terms and as a percent of GDP — this topic is likely to go largely ignored in the 2020 presidential election cycle. Back in 2016, I predicted that no matter who won the presidential election, the national debt was likely to rise. And so it has.

Back in February 2016, MarketWatch reported that "not one presidential candidate cares about the debt and deficits."[6] By July 2016, *The Wall Street Journal had* reported that moves to slash the national debt were "gone."[7] A similar dynamic is likely in the 2020 presidential election, where debt issues go unaddressed.

2017 Tax Reform in Context

U.S. tax reform legislation that was passed in 2017 was lauded as a once-in-a-generation tax cut, which it was. While the reforms changed taxation laws, limits, and brackets for many different kinds of taxes, the legislation did not address entitlements. And payroll taxes were never discussed. Yet some of the biggest risks to the national debt and the long-term potential GDP growth of the U.S. economy will hinge on gaining control over entitlements expenditures and fighting to contain the U.S. national debt. Plus, to cover ballooning entitlements expenditures, payroll taxes could rise sharply, which could exacerbate the tax burden on workers, the self-employed, and people in the gig economy.

Without a reform of the entitlement system, increasingly high levels of government debt and changing demographics are likely to drive up interest rates. And a greater level of debt and higher payroll taxes could contribute to an acceleration of automation — and a reduction of jobs for people over time.

Without a proactive approach, this could become unsustainable for the U.S. labor market, economy, and society.

These issues were not addressed by the self-proclaimed fiscally conservative Republican Party when it had control of both chambers of the legislature and the office of the presidency. This leaves me very concerned about prospects for these issues over the next decade. And it makes one thing seem certain: the 2020 presidential election is unlikely to change these issues.

Risks of Debt

The problem with a rising U.S. national debt is that it can drive up interest rates. After all, as the supply of government bonds rises, the price will fall (as in all markets). And for bonds, when prices fall, interest rates rise. This means that, over time, the net interest on U.S. debt is likely to rise. Allocating an increasing percentage of GDP to interest payments is bad for long-term potential U.S. GDP growth.

The risk of recession increases the likelihood that the debt level and the ratio of debt to GDP are likely to rise between 2020 and 2024. Even without a recession, the level of the national debt and the national debt as a percent of GDP are likely to rise significantly during the current presidential tenure.

And entitlements are a major source of additional imminent debt.

Unfortunately, while the U.S. national debt is large, the unfunded financial obligations stemming from U.S. entitlements is much larger — and it is likely to compound U.S. debt problems in coming years. Simply put, entitlements pose the greatest threat to future U.S. government debt levels — and U.S. economic growth.

Entitlements

U.S. entitlements, including Medicare, Medicaid, and Social Security, are financed by payroll taxes from workers. Payroll taxes are separate from income taxes, and while income tax rates have fallen on fiscal policy changes, payroll taxes are on a one-way trip higher. You see, entitlements are wildly underfunded.

All the sovereign debt in the world totals around $60 trillion.[8] That is the debt cumulatively held by all national governments in the world. But the size of unfunded U.S. entitlements might be more than three times that level. That's right: the unfunded, off-balance sheet obligations for Medicare, Medicaid, and Social Security could be $200 trillion.[9]

This level of off-balance sheet debt obligation existentially threatens the U.S. economy. The Heritage Foundation has taken calculations from the U.S. Congressional Budget Office about entitlements to create Figure 14-3, which looks quite catastrophic. Basically, by 2030, all U.S. tax revenue will be consumed by entitlements and the interest on the national debt. And these were the dismal calculations before tax reform and recent U.S. budgets started increasing the national debt even more rapidly.

The year 2030 is not that far in the future, and the clock is ticking.

But despite the magnitude of the entitlements problem, do not expect this to be an issue that will be seriously addressed during or following the 2020 presidential election.

The Grandfather of U.S. Social Security

Part of the problem with entitlements stems from their origins. The U.S. Social Security Administration website credits Otto von Bismarck as the grandfather of U.S. entitlements.[10] Bismarck's portrait is even on the U.S. Social Security Administration's website (Figure 14-4).

Figure 14-3: Tax Revenue Spent on Entitlements[11]

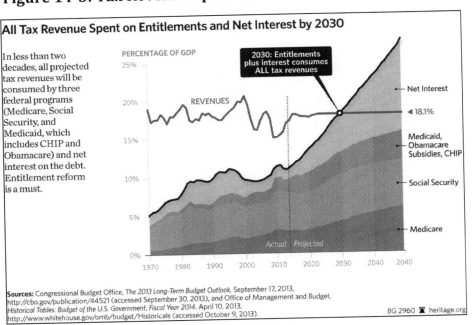

Bismarck was a powerful politician known for his use of *Realpolitik*, a political doctrine built on pragmatism to advance national self interests. For him, entitlements were convenient and expedient. Unfortunately, that is no longer the case. Today, entitlements threaten to crush the U.S. economy with increased levels of debt. And without reform, they could decimate the U.S. workforce.

Bismarck's system was also sustainable. His system guaranteed a pension to German workers over 70, but the average life expectancy in Germany in the late 1880s was only 40.[12] In other words, so few people were expected to receive the benefits that the program's cost would be negligible.

Figure 14-4: Grandfather of Social Security, Otto von Bismarck[13]

Bismarck rigged entitlements to help crush his political opponents without having to pay out. But the current entitlement system in the United States is an unfunded liability that threatens to crush the entire economy and usher in a labor market "Robocalypse." Plus, fixing entitlements presents a horrible dilemma as many Americans rely heavily on entitlements for income (Figure 14-5).

But how did this system break down? Bismarck had such a good thing going. What happened?

This can be answered in one word: demographics.

Figure 14-5: Expected Importance of Social Security[14]

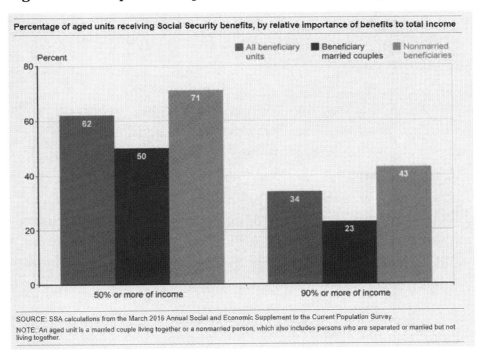

Percentage of aged units receiving Social Security benefits, by relative importance of benefits to total income

SOURCE: SSA calculations from the March 2016 Annual Social and Economic Supplement to the Current Population Survey.
NOTE: An aged unit is a married couple living together or a nonmarried person, which also includes persons who are separated or married but not living together.

Demographics

U.S. population growth has slowed sharply, and this demographic shift appears unstoppable. Plus, as birthrates have fallen, life expectancy has also risen. This compounds the funding shortfalls for entitlements. Worse still: no president, senator, or congressman can change U.S. demographics. This is bigger than one person.

And its discussion is unlikely to be anywhere near the midterm elections.

Population growth in the United States has fallen from annual rates of over 1.5 percent per year during the 1950s and early 1960s to just 0.7 percent since 2011.[15] Some of this slowing in population growth is due to a decline in the U.S. fertility rate. In general, fertility rates have been dropping globally, but according to demographer Jonathan Last, the U.S. fertility rate is still relatively high at 1.93.[16]

However, even though the U.S. total fertility rate is relatively high compared to other industrialized nations, it is below the 2.1 percent "golden number" required to maintain a population, according to Last.[17]

This is a huge problem for maintaining entitlements. After all, the entitlement system worked really well in 1940, when there were 159.4 workers per beneficiary (Figure 14-6), but it is more challenging since that number fell to only 2.8 in 2013. Plus, it is likely to fall to 2 workers per beneficiary by 2040.[18]

Entitlements are under siege from both sides: the birthrate has fallen — and life expectancy has risen.

In addition to lower birthrates, U.S. life expectancy has doubled since Bismarck implemented entitlements in Germany in 1889 — from around 40 years to above 80 years. Plus, the age at which people receive entitlements benefits has actually been lowered from 70 to 65. On top of a significantly larger population being eligible to receive entitlements, the medical costs required to support an aging population have also risen.

Figure 14-6: Ratio of Workers to Social Security Beneficiaries[19]

Year	Covered Workers (in thousands)	Beneficiaries (in thousands)	Ratio
1940	35,390	222	159.4
1945	46,390	1,106	41.9
1950	48,280	2,930	16.5
1955	65,200	7,563	8.6
1960	72,530	14,262	5.1
1965	80,680	20,157	4.0
1970	93,090	25,186	3.7
1975	100,200	31,123	3.2
1980	113,656	35,118	3.2
1985	120,565	36,650	3.3
1990	133,672	39,470	3.4
1995	141,446	43,107	3.3
2000	155,295	45,166	3.4
2005	159,081	48,133	3.3
2010	156,725	53,398	2.9
2013	163,221	57,471	2.8

Everything might be OK — if U.S. population growth were extremely robust. But it is not. Plus, the current administration is pushing hard to reduce illegal immigration to the United States. While this can have some benefits for society and the economy in some ways, it can also reduce the pace of population growth and lower the average U.S. birthrate.

Population growth has slowed to less than half the rate seen during the baby boom years, and the total U.S. fertility rate is below the "golden number" that is required to maintain a population. As Last notes, "Social Security is, in essence, a Ponzi scheme. Like all Ponzi schemes, it works just fine — so long as the intake of new participants continues to increase."[20] Unfortunately, entitlements are nearing a breaking point.

A big problem with slowing birthrates is the manifestation of a shrinking tax base at the same time that unfunded financial obligations are rising. This means that the unfunded $200 trillion or more in future entitlements payments will be borne by an increasingly smaller proportion of the population. And as the population ages, there is another issue: who will do the work? The answer is simple: we will create jobs for robots.

Payroll Taxes and a Shrinking U.S. Tax Base
When there is a tax shortfall, there is often a need to raise taxes. And there are risks of significantly higher payroll taxes in the not-too-distant future. Slowing population growth is likely to exacerbate U.S. debt and entitlement burdens by accelerating the reduction in the U.S. tax base — especially for payroll taxes, which fund entitlements. This could justify raising payroll taxes.

So, who pays payroll taxes?

Employees split entitlement costs with their employers, who pay half. This means that if entitlement costs rise, the cost for an employer to keep a person employed will also increase. The substitution effect of automation for labor would then likely accelerate because of the financial incentives in place for employers.

As payroll taxes increase to cover the costs associated with underfunded entitlements, the financial incentives for employers to shift work away from human laborers and add technology are likely to be reinforced. A number of my clients have shared their concerns about the risk of rising costs associated with health care costs for their workers.

How do you think employers will feel about the burden of paying much higher payroll taxes? They do pay half of them, after all.

Automation

As U.S. population growth slows, and older workers age out of the workforce, automation could provide a solution. Automation has the potential to contribute significantly to U.S. economic growth.

But while automation solves some of the demographic problems we have in the United States, it threatens to exacerbate some of the entitlement problems. And unreformed entitlements present a significant risk of over-automation to the U.S. economy. If you were to think of the most important benefits you get as an employee, you might think of time off or sick days.

But your employer probably thinks about the most expensive items first: payroll taxes and health care. Kiosks don't get time off, they certainly don't require health care costs, and they aren't subject to payroll taxes — for now.

In mid-2016, unemployment in Spain was around 20 percent,[21] and youth unemployment was around 43 percent.[22] So there were a lot of people available to work. But in Barcelona, Spain, during the summer of 2016, kiosks were in use at the airport's Burger King restaurant.

In Spain, as in much of Europe, the cost to hire someone can be prohibitive compared to the United States. And these kiosks require no payroll taxes, no health insurance costs, no government entitlements, no vacation, and no sick days. With these kinds of kiosks replacing workers, youth unemployment is unlikely to get significantly better. This also bodes ill for U.S. youth participation and unemployment rates. Be advised: fast food robots (among others) are coming.

Entrepreneurs at Risk
Rising entitlement costs and payroll taxes could also stifle entrepreneurship. Unlike employees, who split payroll tax obligations with their employers, self-employed people bear the full brunt of payroll taxes personally. The rate is currently 15.3 percent of income.[23] In the future, that rate will rise faster for entrepreneurs since they will not be splitting the increase in payroll taxes with an employer. If entitlements are not drastically overhauled, a self-employment tax rate of 25 percent by 2030 is not inconceivable.

Increasingly high self-employment tax rates are likely to stifle entrepreneurship and hurt self-employed workers. According to an article by the Pew Foundation, the percent of workers who are self-employed fell from 11.4 percent in 1990 to 10 percent in 2014.[24] More importantly, the Pew Foundation notes that 30 percent of U.S. jobs are held "by the self-employed and the workers they hire."[25] In other words, in 2014, 14.6 million self-employed workers hired another 29.4 million workers, making 30 percent of employees.

With the prospect of entitlement shortfalls and a shrinking tax base, self-employment tax rates are going to rise. The impact of these additional costs is likely to engender a continued downward trend in the percent of self-employed workers. Plus, workers in the so-called gig economy — like all 1099s — are also subject to self-employment taxes. This could also make the existence of the gig economy less tenable as payroll taxes rise.

The labor force participation rate is also at risk as we see the population aging, unfunded entitlements rising, and the potential for overincentivized automation.

The labor force participation rate is a measure of what percentage of the able-bodied civilian population is working or looking for work. I also expect youth participation rates will continue to fall as younger workers are crowded out by older workers and automation.

Other Unfunded Obligations

As tax incentives present risks that workers could be crowded out by automation, consider also that the $200 trillion figure for unfunded entitlements does not take into account pension data for federal, state, county, or city government employees. Many of these workers also have defined benefits pensions that are underfunded — and in great need of reform. The gap in funds for these pensions will also likely incentivize automation and drive jobs for robots — rather than jobs for people.

There is an old joke that the best kind of autoworker to be is a retired autoworker. Without a reform of entitlements and defined benefits plans, the joke could be rewritten that the best kind of any U.S. worker to be will be a retired U.S. worker. This will affect all of us since unfunded off-balance sheet obligations could necessitate that government and private pension benefits be drastically reduced (especially for future generations) while contribution costs rise further. Problems beget problems.

Challenges to Progress

With challenges ahead, one might hope for more progress. But presidents consistently have less success in Congress as their terms progress, as indicated in Figure 14-7. This means that a rising percentage of initiatives that the president supports are likely to find more resistance in Congress in coming years.

The reason for this decline may be that the president spends political capital earlier in his tenure. Or perhaps this decline is a function of midterm elections that typically result in a loss of seats in the legislature from the president's party.

Whatever the case, this trend was likely to continue with President Trump after the 2018 midterm elections. And it did. If Trump is reelected in 2020, it could continue further.

Conversely, if a Democratic challenger unseats Trump as U.S. president, there may a blue wave of votes that also gives the Democrats more legislative control. This would likely start the cycle all over again, with higher success early in the term of a new president.

But entitlements reform and cutting government spending may not be at the top of a new Democratic president's docket. It will depend heavily on who gets the nomination.

Figure 14-7: President Success Declines During Tenure[26]

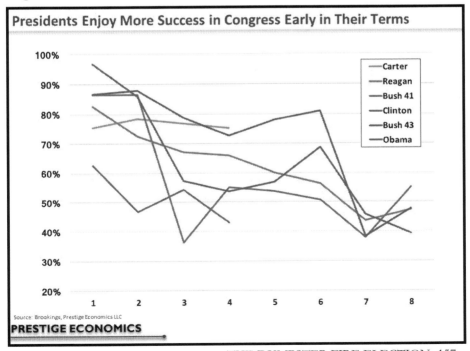

Presidents Enjoy More Success in Congress Early in Their Terms

Source: Brookings, Prestige Economics LLC

PRESTIGE ECONOMICS

In fact, some Democrats, like 2020 presidential-hopeful Andrew Yang, have started advocating for Universal Basic Income, which would essentially be free money for everyone. I have written about this at length in my book *Jobs for Robots*. Needless to say, it would greatly increase the risk of even more government debt.

Summary

Rising debt levels in the United States present long-term risks to growth. The surprise with the 2017 tax cuts was that despite Republican stewardship of the initiative, they were unbalanced. As an economist, I see tax cuts as good. But I also see more debt as bad. Unfortunately, the tax reform of 2017 included both tax cuts — and more debt.

Plus, the most recent budgets during the current term of the Trump administration also included significant increases in the national debt. This means that even if Trump is reelected president, there may still be a need to "pork up" future budgets.

In the longer-term, declines in birthrates, increased longevity, rising health care costs, falling labor force participation rates, and overincentivized automation are likely to accelerate and exacerbate the problems of the U.S. national defined benefits programs known as entitlements — programs that worked best financially when the age at which one received benefits exceeded life expectancy by 30 years.

But the entitlements system was ignored during the 2016 presidential election, during the 2017 tax reform, and in the 2018 midterms. It is likely to remain ignored for as long as possible — and likely through the 2020 presidential election cycle.

CHAPTER 15

RESPONDING TO
RISKS AND CHALLENGES

It is important to have a plan for how you will react to the risks and challenges ahead. After all, as you have seen in this book, some of the most important economic and financial market risks that lie ahead for the average person are not dependent on which party controls the White House, let alone which party controls Congress. The most important issues have already been set in stone: Fed policy, the rising national debt, unreformed entitlements, and demographics present significant, if not existential, threats to the U.S. economy.

Trendline Over Headline
The steady stream of U.S. economic data is critical for presidential candidates ahead of an election, and they fill Twitter feeds and blog posts. But these changes in the U.S. economy can be minor compared to some of the larger risks I have discussed in the previous chapter. An economist I used to work with liked to say that the economy often looked good on the surface, but tectonic plates underneath threatened to upend the apparent calm. Another way to say this is to look past the headline for a long-term trendline.

Option #1: Get Active

Because some of the biggest risks to the U.S. economy are not on the radar of most politicians, one way to address the issues that concern you is to get civically involved. Regardless of your party affiliation, if these issues concern you, contact your government representatives.

I can't guarantee it, but I expect there is some kind of algorithm politicians use to evaluate constituent sentiment that is influenced by touch points. In other words, when you reach out, there is a kind of leverage for your outreach. There is likely an equation to determine how many people didn't reach out but who also cared about a certain issue.

According to Peter and Hull in *The Peter Principle*: "A political party is usually naively pictured as a group of like-minded people operating to further their common interests. This is no longer valid. That function is now carried on entirely by *the lobby*, and there are as many lobbies as there are special interests."[1] Become one of those special interests. Your political representatives' contact info is here: https://www.usa.gov/elected-officials.

I am involved in multiple political groups, and you should be too!

Option #2: Manage Your Finances

A few years ago, I attended an invitation-only off-site event of the Atlanta Fed, where an expert from a think tank told the high-profile audience that the only way to solve the U.S. debt and entitlements issues was with a two-pronged approach of repression and inflation.

The inflation component of this equation is quite clear, but the repression component may not be. The repression part, he argued, is that the government might eventually mandate that tax -advantaged retirement accounts — like IRAs and 401(k)s — be required to hold government Treasuries. This would open up U.S. debt to an entirely new (and captive) pool of capital — but it could be a disaster for investors.

A former client of mine was a very serious investment banker — one of the top guys in his field. This very serious senior investment banking managing director converted his investments to an annuity because he has more faith in an insurance company to pay out the annuity than he does in the U.S. government not to seize his retirement account at some point. And he may very well be right!

I'm not recommending this,[2] but I think it's critical for you to know that serious people in finance and banking have very real concerns that a government mandate on Treasury purchases is going to happen at some point. If we do not fix the debt and entitlements situation, this is a very real possibility. From a risk management standpoint, annuities and physical assets would be tougher for the U.S. government to seize or direct if it needed to sell more Treasuries. And it *will* need to sell more debt.

As we saw in Chapter 14, by 2030, the entire U.S. tax budget (as a percent of GDP) is expected to cover just the cost of entitlements and the interest on the U.S. national debt.

Option #3: Manage Your Career (and Read *Recession-Proof*)

I spent a great deal of time in my book *Recession-Proof* discussing how to best manage your career — especially in uncertain economic times. No matter how big the economic risks, there are always some industries that will be evergreen.

In light of the aging U.S. population, health care is likely to remain a huge opportunity professionally. While entitlements and demographics may threaten a number of industries with automation, health care is likely to remain evergreen as a more difficult sector to automate for some time to come. In fact, any industry where you need person-to-person contact is likely to remain relatively safe. As such, a career in health care or caregiving is likely to be a solid option for some time.

In addition to the opportunities presented by the health care sector, there are also likely to be significant opportunities in information technology — especially automation. And project management will become a more critical field, even as automation and robots become more integral parts of advanced workforces.

Robots and automation are coming — especially if the national debt and entitlements remain big issues. You need to find a way to benefit from these changes, which I discuss in my book *Robot-Proof Yourself*.

What Will Happen Next?

The 2020 election is 16 months away, and a lot can happen in that time. In President Trump's favor right now are his incumbency, his ability to get eyes on screens, and a strong economy. But if the unemployment rate rises, trade tensions cause growth to slow further, or some other unexpected events shift the voting dynamics of battleground states, he could be in for a fight that could be won by a not-yet-nominated Democratic challenger.

There are many different reasons to vote for a political candidate for president. But from an economic standpoint, you may wish to consider voting for the party that you believe has the highest probability of addressing long-term risks like entitlements, which pose an existential threat to the U.S. economy.

For now, despite the rapid approach of the *election-recession window* and the historical presence of an apparent *term limit on growth*, you should take some solace in the fact that the U.S. economy has been stronger in the year ahead of the 2020 presidential election than it was going into the 2016 presidential election.

Looking beyond 2020, the economic and financial market aftermath of the 2020 presidential election will be driven by tax policy expectations in the short run and by big, scary, unaddressed risks in the long run. But before we get there, political polarization, weaponized social media, and subnational identities are likely to make the process an absolute dumpster fire.

ENDNOTES

INTRODUCTION

1. Schwarz, Hunter. "RIP 'American Idol': The show that proved how bad Americans are at voting." *The Washington Post*, 11 May 2015. Retrieved on 17 June 2019 from https:// www.washingtonpost.com/news/the-fix/wp/2015/05/11/rip-american-idol-the-show-that-gave -us-an-easy-shorthand-for-americans-not-voting/
2. Krasney, Ros. "Trump Warns of Epic Stock Market Crash If He's Not Re-Elected." *Bloomberg*, 15 June 2019. Retrieved on 17 June 2019 from https://www.bloomberg.com/news/articles/2019-06-15/trump -warns-of-epic-stock-market-crash-if-he-s-not-re-elected

CHAPTER 2

1. "List of Political Parties in the United States." *Ballotpedia*, Ballotpedia, ballotpedia.org/ List_of_political_parties_in_the_United_States. June 17, 2019.
2. "Historical Presidential Elections." *Historical U.S. Presidential Elections 1789-2016*, 270towin, www.270towin.com/historical-presidential-elections/. 17 June 2019.
3. Editors, History.com. "Andrew Jackson." *History.com*, A&E Television Networks, 29 Oct. 2009, www.history.com/topics/us-presidents/andrew-jackson.
4. Rudin, Ken. "When Has A President Been Denied His Party's Nomination?" *NPR*, NPR, 22 July 2009, www.npr.org/sections/politicaljunkie/2009/07/a_president_denied_renominatio.html.
5. Ibid.
6. Perticone, Joe. "No Sitting President Has Survived a Serious Primary Challenge in the Past 50 Years. Here's Why Trump Should Be Worried." *Business Insider*, Business Insider, 7 March 2019, www.businessinsider.com/sitting-presidents-serious-primary-challenges-often-lose-reelection-2019-3.
7. Jones, Jeffrey M. "Lieberman Continues to Pace Democratic Field." *Gallup.com*, Gallup Inc., 25 June 2003, news.gallup.com/poll/8716/lieberman-continues-pace-democratic-field.aspx.
8. Jones, Jeffrey M., et al. "Where the Election Stands: June 2007." *Gallup.com*, Gallup Inc., 27 June 2007, news.gallup.com/poll/27985/where-election-stands-june-2007.aspx.
9. Jones, Jeffrey M. "Romney Support Up; Widens Advantage in 2012 Preferences." *Gallup.com*, Gallup Inc., 13 June 2011, news.gallup.com/poll/148016/romney-support-widens-advantage-2012-preferences.aspx.
10. Quinnipiac University. "QU Poll Release Detail." *QU Poll*, Quinnipiac University, 15 April 2015, poll.qu.edu/national/release-detail?ReleaseID=2221.
11. Dugan, Andrew. "Among Republicans, GOP Candidates Better Known Than Liked." *Gallup.com*, Gallup Inc., 24 July 2015, news.gallup.com/poll/184337/among-republicans-gop-candidates-better-known-liked.aspx.
12. Dugan, Andrew, and Justin McCarthy. "Hillary Clinton Clear Leader in Favorability Among Democrats." *Gallup.com*, Gallup Inc., 13 March 2015, news.gallup.com/poll/181988/hillary-clinton -clear-leader-favorability-among-democrats.aspx.
13. Sparks, Grace. "Top 2020 Democrats Best Trump in Hypothetical Matchups in New Poll." *CNN*, Cable News Network, 11 June 2019, www.cnn.com/2019/06/11/politics/2020-matchups-quinnipiac-poll/index.html?no-st=1560811232.
14. "Joe Biden." *Wikipedia*, Wikimedia Foundation, 17 June 2019, en.wikipedia.org/wiki/ Joe_Biden.
15. "Bernie Sanders." *Wikipedia*, Wikimedia Foundation, 16 June 2019, en.wikipedia.org/wiki/ Bernie_Sanders.
16. "2020 Presidential Election Interactive Map." *270toWin.Com*, 270towin.com , www.270towin.com/. Retrieved on 17 June 2019.
17. Parlapiano, Alicia and Adam Pearce "Only 9% of America Chose Trump and Clinton as the Nominees." *New York Times*, 1 August 2016. Retrieved from http://www.nytimes.com/ interactive/2016/08/01/us/elections/nine-percent-of-america-selected-trump-and-clinton.html

CHAPTER 3

1. Pillsbury, George, and Julian Johannesen. "America Goes to the Polls 2016." Nonprofit Vote, 1 March 2017, p. 13. Retrieved from www.nonprofitvote.org/america-goes-to-the-polls-2016.
2. Ibid.

CHAPTER 4

1. Kapur, Sahil. "These 20 Democrats Have Qualified for the First Presidential Debate." *Bloomberg.com*, Bloomberg, 13 June 2019, www.bloomberg.com/news/articles/2019-06-13/20-candidates-qualify-first-democratic-debate.
2. Dovere, Edward-Isaac. "The Democratic Clown Car Rolls Into Iowa." *The Atlantic*, Atlantic Media Company, 10 June 2019, www.theatlantic.com/politics/archive/2019/06/democrats-campaign-iowa/591328/.
3. Rauch, Jonathan. "How American Politics Went Insane." *The Atlantic*, Atlantic Media Company, 19 April 2018, www.theatlantic.com/magazine/archive/2016/07/how-american-politics-went-insane/485570.
4. Ibid.
5. Ibid.
6. Silver, Nate. "How Much Did Russian Interference Affect The 2016 Election?" *FiveThirtyEight*, ABC, 16 Feb. 2018, fivethirtyeight.com/features/how-much-did-russian-interference-affect-the-2016-election/. See also United States of America v. Internet Research Agency LLC et al., 18 U.S.C. §§ 2, 371, 1349, 1028A (2018)
7. Silver, Nate. "How Much Did Russian Interference Affect The 2016 Election?" *FiveThirtyEight*, ABC, 16 Feb. 2018, fivethirtyeight.com/features/how-much-did-russian-interference-affect-the-2016-election/.
8. Isaac, Mike, and Daisuke Wakabayashi. "Russian Influence Reached 126 Million Through Facebook Alone." *The New York Times*, The New York Times, 30 Oct. 2017, www.nytimes.com/2017/10/30/technology/facebook-google-russia.html?save=nyt-gateway-stories.
9. Silver, Nate. "How Much Did Russian Interference Affect The 2016 Election?" *FiveThirtyEight*, ABC, 16 Feb. 2018, fivethirtyeight.com/features/how-much-did-russian-interference-affect-the-2016-election/.
10. Turton, William. "We Posed as 100 Senators to Run Ads on Facebook. Facebook Approved All of Them." *VICE News*, VICE News, 30 Oct. 2018, news.vice.com/en_ca/article/xw9n3q/we-posed-as-100-senators-to-run-ads-on-facebook-facebook-approved-all-of-them.
11. Ibid.
12. Benedict Anderson, *Imagined Communities*, (New York: Verso, 1991), 43. Also pp. 6, 26-27.

CHAPTER 5

1. "Political Polarization in the American Public." *Pew Research Center for the People and the Press*, Pew Research Center, 11 Oct. 2016, www.people-press.org/2014/06/12/political-polarization-in-the-american-public/.
2. Ibid.
3. Ibid.
4. Ibid.
5. Ibid.
6. Ibid.
7. Ibid.
8. Ibid.
9. Mitchell, Amy, et al. "Political Polarization & Media Habits." *Pew Research Center's Journalism Project*, Pew Research Center, 26 April 2018, www.journalism.org/2014/10/21/political-polarization-media-habits/.
10. "Political Polarization in the American Public." *Pew Research Center for the People and the Press*, Pew Research Center, 11 October 2016, www.people-press.org/2014/06/12/political-polarization-in-the-american-public/.

11. Edkins, Brett. "Report: U.S. Media Among Most Polarized In The World." *Forbes*, Forbes Magazine, 27 June 2017, www.forbes.com/sites/brettedkins/2017/06/27/u-s-media-among-most-polarized-in-the-world-study-finds/#53c86bde2546.

CHAPTER 6
1. Amadeo, Kimberly. "Compare Today's Unemployment With the Past." *The Balance*, The Balance, 21 May 2019, www.thebalance.com/unemployment-rate-by-year-3305506.

CHAPTER 7
1. Narayanswamy, Anu, et al. "How Much Money Is behind Each Campaign?" *The Washington Post*, WP Company, 1 Feb. 2016, www.washingtonpost.com/graphics/politics/2016-election/campaign-finance/?noredirect=on.
2. Mercer, Andrew, et al. "Why 2016 Election Polls Missed Their Mark." *FactTank News in the Numbers*, Pew Research Center, 9 Nov. 2016, www.pewresearch.org/fact-tank/2016/11/09/why-2016-election-polls-missed-their-mark/. See also Shepard, Steven. "GOP Insiders: Polls Don't Capture Secret Trump Vote." *The POLITICO Caucus*, POLITICO, 28 Oct. 2016, www.politico.com/story/2016/10/donald-trump-shy-voters-polls-gop-insiders-230411.
3. Bond, Paul. "Leslie Moonves on Donald Trump: 'It May Not Be Good for America, but It's Damn Good for CBS.'" *The Hollywood Reporter*, The Hollywood Reporter, 1 March 2016, www.hollywoodreporter.com/news/leslie-moonves-donald-trump-may-871464.
4. Ibid.
5. Hibberd, James. "Donald Trump Gives 'SNL' Biggest Ratings in Years." *EW.com*, Entertainment Weekly, 8 Nov. 2015, ew.com/article/2015/11/08/donald-trump-snl-ratings/.

CHAPTER 8
1. Stark, Caitlin. "By the Numbers: Second Term Presidents - CNNPolitics." *CNN*, Cable News Network, 9 Nov. 2012, www.cnn.com/2012/11/09/politics/btn-second-term-presidents/index.html?no-st=1560814097.
2. Ibid.
3. Ibid.

CHAPTER 9
1. *Prestige Economics Quarterly Benchmarking, July 2016*. Prestige Economics.
2. *Prestige Economics Quarterly Benchmarking, April 2019*. Prestige Economics.
3. Federal Reserve Economic Database, FRED, Federal Reserve Bank of St. Louis: https://fred.stlouisfed.org/ .
4. U.S. Bureau of Economic Analysis, Gross Domestic Product [GDP], retrieved from FRED, Federal Reserve Bank of St. Louis; https://fred.stlouisfed.org/series/GDP, June 17, 2019.
5. U.S. Bureau of Economic Analysis, Real Gross Domestic Product [GDPC1], retrieved from FRED, Federal Reserve Bank of St. Louis; https://fred.stlouisfed.org/series/GDPC1, June 17, 2019.
6. U.S. Bureau of Labor Statistics, Civilian Unemployment Rate [UNRATE], retrieved from FRED, Federal Reserve Bank of St. Louis; https://fred.stlouisfed.org/series/UNRATE, June 17, 2019.
7. U.S. Bureau of Labor Statistics, Consumer Price Index for All Urban Consumers: All Items [CPIAUCSL], retrieved from FRED, Federal Reserve Bank of St. Louis; https://fred.stlouisfed.org/series/CPIAUCSL, June 17, 2019.
8. Board of Governors of the Federal Reserve System (U.S.), Industrial Production Index [INDPRO], retrieved from FRED, Federal Reserve Bank of St. Louis; https://fred.stlouisfed.org/series/INDPRO, June 17, 2019.
9. Institute of Supply Management. Data sourced from econoday.com.
10. U.S. Bureau of the Census, Advance Retail Sales: Retail (Excluding Food Services) [RSXFS], retrieved from FRED, Federal Reserve Bank of St. Louis; https://fred.stlouisfed.org/series/RSXFS, June 17, 2019.
11. U.S. Bureau of Economic Analysis, Light Weight Vehicle Sales: Autos and Light Trucks [ALTSALES], retrieved from FRED, Federal Reserve Bank of St. Louis; https://fred.stlouisfed.org/series/ALTSALES, June 17, 2019.

12. U.S. Bureau of the Census, Housing Starts: Total: New Privately Owned Housing Units Started [HOUST], retrieved from FRED, Federal Reserve Bank of St. Louis; https://fred.stlouisfed.org/series/HOUST, June 17, 2019.
13. Board of Governors of the Federal Reserve System (U.S.), Effective Federal Funds Rate [DFF], retrieved from FRED, Federal Reserve Bank of St. Louis; https://fred.stlouisfed.org/series/DFF, June 17, 2019.
14. Chinese Manufacturing PMI data sourced from www.econoday.com.
15. Eurozone Manufacturing PMI data sourced from www.econoday.com.
16. Retrieved from www.imf.org.

CHAPTER 10
1. S&P Dow Jones Indices LLC, Dow Jones Industrial Average© [DJIA], retrieved from FRED, Federal Reserve Bank of St. Louis; https://fred.stlouisfed.org/series/DJIA, June 17, 2019.
2. S&P Dow Jones Indices LLC, S&P 500© [SP500], retrieved from FRED, Federal Reserve Bank of St. Louis; https://fred.stlouisfed.org/series/SP500, June 17, 2019.
3. Board of Governors of the Federal Reserve System (U.S.), Real Trade Weighted US Dollar Index: Major Currencies [TWEXMPA], retrieved from FRED, Federal Reserve Bank of St. Louis; https://fred.stlouisfed.org/series/TWEXMPA, June 17, 2019.
4. Ibid.
5. London Bullion Market Association as sourced from MacroTrends Data. Additional data sourced from eSignal.
6. London Bullion Market Association as sourced from MacroTrends Data. Additional data sourced from eSignal.
7. Energy Information Administration, Bureau of Labor Statistics as sourced from MacroTrends Data. Additional data sourced from eSignal.

CHAPTER 11
1. "US Business Cycle Expansions and Contractions." *The National Bureau of Economic Research*, NBER, 20 Sept. 2010, www.nber.org/cycles.html.
2. "About the NBER." *The National Bureau of Economic Research*, NBER, www.nber.org/info.html. 17 June 2019.
3. Analysis performed from: "US Business Cycle Expansions and Contractions." *The National Bureau of Economic Research*, NBER, 20 Sept. 2010, www.nber.org/cycles.html.

CHAPTER 12
1. U.S. Bureau of Labor Statistics, Civilian Unemployment Rate [UNRATE], retrieved from FRED, Federal Reserve Bank of St. Louis; https://fred.stlouisfed.org/series/UNRATE, 17 June 2019.
2. Ibid.
3. Board of Governors of the Federal Reserve System (U.S.), Industrial Production Index [INDPRO], retrieved from FRED, Federal Reserve Bank of St. Louis; https://fred.stlouisfed.org/series/INDPRO, 17 June 2019.
4. U.S. Bureau of the Census, Housing Starts: Total: New Privately Owned Housing Units Started [HOUST], retrieved from FRED, Federal Reserve Bank of St. Louis; https://fred.stlouisfed.org/series/HOUST, 17 June 2019.
5. U.S. Bureau of Economic Analysis, Light Weight Vehicle Sales: Autos and Light Trucks [ALTSALES], retrieved from FRED, Federal Reserve Bank of St. Louis; https://fred.stlouisfed.org/series/ALTSALES, 17 June 2019.

CHAPTER 13
1. S&P Dow Jones Indices LLC, Dow Jones Industrial Average© [DJIA], retrieved from FRED, Federal Reserve Bank of St. Louis; https://fred.stlouisfed.org/series/DJIA, 17 June 2019.
2. Board of Governors of the Federal Reserve System (US), Real Trade Weighted U.S. Dollar Index: Major Currencies [TWEXMPA], retrieved from FRED, Federal Reserve Bank of St. Louis; https://fred.stlouisfed.org/series/TWEXMPA, 17 June 2019.

3. London Bullion Market Association, Bureau of Labor Statistics as sourced from MacroTrends Data.

4. London Bullion Market Association, Bureau of Labor Statistics as sourced from MacroTrends Data.

5. Energy Information Administration, Bureau of Labor Statistics as sourced from MacroTrends Data.

6. Ibid.

CHAPTER 14

1. Yellen, Janet. *"The Federal Reserve's Monetary Policy Toolkit: Past, Present, and Future."* 26 August 2016. US Federal Reserve. Retrieved from https://www.federalreserve.gov/newsevents/speech/yellen20160826a.htm

2. Retrieved from http://www.usdebtclock.org/

3. U.S. Department of the Treasury. Fiscal Service, Federal Debt: Total Public Debt [GFDEBTN], retrieved from FRED, Federal Reserve Bank of St. Louis; https://fred.stlouisfed.org/series/GFDEBTN, 17 June 2019.

4. Ibid.

5. Federal Reserve Bank of St. Louis and US Office of Management and Budget, Federal Debt: Total Public Debt as Percent of Gross Domestic Product [GFDEGDQ188S], retrieved from FRED, Federal Reserve Bank of St. Louis; https://fred.stlouisfed.org/series/GFDEGDQ188S, 17 June 2019.

6. Gold, Howard. "Not one presidential candidate cares about the debt and deficits," *Marketwatch*, 3 February 2016. Retrieved from http://www.marketwatch.com/story/not-one-presidential-candidate-cares-about-the-debt-and-deficits-2016-02-03.

7. Timiraos, Nick. "Debate Over U.S. Debt Changes Tone," *The Wall Street Journal*, 24 July 2016. Retrieved from http://www.wsj.com/articles/debate-over-u-s-debt-changes-tone-1469385857.

8. Desjardins, J. (6 August 2015). "$60 Trillion of World Debt in One Visualization." Visual Capitalist. Retrieved 11 February 2017: http://www.visualcapitalist.com/60-trillion-of-world-debt-in-one-visualization/.

9. Mayer, J. (18 November 2015). "The Social Security Façade." Retrieved 11 February 2017: http://www.usnews.com/opinion/economic-intelligence/2015/11/18/social-security-and-medicare-have-morphed-into-unsustainable-entitlements.

10. US Social Security Administration. "Social Security History: Otto von Bismarck." Sourced from https://www.ssa.gov/history/ottob.html.

11. Image provided courtesy of The Heritage Foundation. Retrieved 11 February 2017: http://thf_media.s3.amazonaws.com/infographics/2014/10/BG-eliminate-waste-control-spending-chart-3_HIGHRES.jpg.

12. Twarog, S. (January 1997). "Heights and Living Standards in Germany, 1850-1939: The Case of Wurttemberg" as reprinted in *Health and Welfare During Industrialization*. Steckel, R. and F. Roderick, eds. Chicago: University of Chicago Press, p. 315. Retrieved 11 February 2017: http://www.nber.org/chapters/c7434.pdf.

13. U.S. Social Security Administration. "Social Security History: Otto von Bismarck." Sourced from https://www.ssa.gov/history/ottob.html.

14. U.S. Social Security Administration. *Fast Facts and Figures About Social Security, 2017*, p. 8. Retrieved on 17 June 2019: https://www.ssa.gov/policy/docs/chartbooks/fast_facts/.

15. World Bank, Population Growth for the United States [SPPOPGROWUSA], retrieved from FRED, Federal Reserve Bank of St. Louis; https://fred.stlouisfed.org/series/SPPOPGROWUSA, June 5, 2018.

16. Last, J. (2013) *What to Expect, When No One's Expecting: America's Coming Demographic Disaster*. New York: Encounter Books., pp. 2-4.

17. Ibid., p. 3.

18. Last (2013), p. 109.

19. Social Security Administration. Retrieved 11 February 2017 from https://www.ssa.gov/history/ratios.html Last (2013) also uses a similar table in his book on p. 108.

20. Last (2013), p. 107.

21. Trading Economics. Spanish unemployment. Retrieved February 2017 http:// www.tradingeconomics.com/spain/unemployment-rate.

22. Trading Economics. Spanish unemployment. Retrieved February 2017 http:// www.tradingeconomics.com/spain/youth-unemployment-rate.

23. U.S. Internal Revenue Service. Retrieved from https://www.irs.gov/businesses/small-businesses-self-employed/self-employment-tax-social-security-and-medicare-taxes.

24. Pew Research Center. (22 October 2015). Retrieved 19 February 2017: http:// www.pewsocialtrends.org/2015/10/22/three-in-ten-u-s-jobs-are-held-by-the-self-employed-and -the-workers-they-hire/.

25. Ibid.

26. "Vital Statistics on Congress." The Brookings Institution, 22 May 2018. Retrieved from www.brookings.edu/multi-chapter-report/vital-statistics-on-congress/

CHAPTER 15

1. Peter and Hull (2009), p. 58.

2. I am actually not making any explicit recommendations or giving investment advice. Please see the disclaimers in the back of the book.

ABOUT THE AUTHOR

Jason Schenker is the President of Prestige Economics and the world's top-ranked financial market futurist. Bloomberg News has ranked Mr. Schenker the #1 forecaster in the world in 25 categories since 2011, including for his forecasts of crude oil prices, natural gas prices, the euro, the pound, the Swiss franc, the Chinese RMB, gold prices, industrial metals prices, agricultural prices, U.S. non-farm payrolls, and U.S. home sales.

Mr. Schenker has written 16 books and edited two almanacs. Five of his books have been #1 Bestsellers on Amazon, including *Commodity Prices 101*, *Recession-Proof*, *Electing Recession*, *Quantum: Computing Nouveau*, and *Jobs for Robots*. He also edited the #1 Best Seller *The Robot and Automation Almanac — 2018* as well as the 2019 edition of the almanac. Mr. Schenker is also a columnist for *Bloomberg Opinion*, and he has appeared as a guest host on Bloomberg Television as well as a guest on CNBC and other television media. He is frequently quoted in the press, including *The Wall Street Journal*, *The New York Times*, and *The Financial Times*.

Prior to founding Prestige Economics, Mr. Schenker worked for McKinsey & Company as a Risk Specialist, where he directed trading and risk initiatives on six continents. Before joining McKinsey, Mr. Schenker worked for Wachovia as an Economist.

Mr. Schenker holds a Master's in Applied Economics from UNC Greensboro, a Master's in Negotiation from CSU Dominguez Hills, a Master's in German from UNC Chapel Hill, and a Bachelor's with distinction in History and German from The University of Virginia. He also holds a certificate in FinTech from MIT, an executive certificate in Supply Chain Management from MIT, a graduate certificate in Professional Development from UNC, a certificate in Negotiation from Harvard Law School, and a certificate in Cybersecurity from Carnegie Mellon University.

Mr. Schenker holds the professional designations ERP® (Energy Risk Professional), CMT® (Chartered Market Technician), CVA® (Certified Valuation Analyst), CFP® (Certified Financial Planner), and FLTA™ (Certified Futurist and Long-Term Analyst). Mr. Schenker is also an instructor for LinkedIn Learning. His courses include Financial Risk Management, Recession-Proof Strategies, Audit and Due Diligence, and a weekly Economic Indicator Series.

Mr. Schenker is a member of the Texas Business Leadership Council, the only CEO-based public policy research organization in Texas, with a limited membership of 100 CEOs and Presidents. He is also a 2018 Board of Director member of the Texas Lyceum, a non-partisan, nonprofit that fosters business and policy dialogue on important U.S. and Texas issues. He is also the VP of Technology for the Texas Lyceum Executive Committee.

Mr. Schenker is an active executive in FinTech. He has been a member of the Central Texas Angel Network, and he advises multiple startups and nonprofits. He is also a member of the National Association of Corporate Directors as well as an NACD Board Governance Fellow.

In October 2016, Mr. Schenker founded The Futurist Institute to help consultants, strategists, and executives become futurists through an online and in-person training and certification program. Participants can earn the Certified Futurist and Long-Term Analyst™ — FLTA™ — designation.

Mr. Schenker was ranked one of the top 100 most influential financial advisors in the world by Investopedia in June 2018.

For more information about Jason Schenker:
www.jasonschenker.com

For more information about The Futurist Institute:
www.futuristinstitute.org

For more information about Prestige Economics:
www.prestigeeconomics.com

TOP FORECASTER ACCURACY RANKINGS

Prestige Economics has been recognized as the most accurate independent commodity and financial market research firm in the world. As the only forecaster for Prestige Economics, Jason Schenker is very proud that Bloomberg News has ranked him a top forecaster in 43 different categories since 2011, including #1 in the world in 25 different forecast categories.

Mr. Schenker has been top ranked as a forecaster of economic indicators, energy prices, metals prices, agricultural prices, and foreign exchange rates.

ECONOMIC TOP RANKINGS
#1 Non-Farm Payroll Forecaster in the World
#1 New Home Sales Forecaster in the World
#2 U.S. Unemployment Rate Forecaster in the World
#3 Durable Goods Orders Forecaster in the World
#6 Consumer Confidence Forecaster in the World
#7 ISM Manufacturing Index Forecaster in the World
#7 U.S. Housing Start Forecaster in the World

ENERGY PRICE TOP RANKINGS
#1 WTI Crude Oil Price Forecaster in the World
#1 Brent Crude Oil Price Forecaster in the World
#1 Henry Hub Natural Gas Price Forecaster in the World

METALS PRICE TOP RANKINGS
#1 Gold Price Forecaster in the World
#1 Platinum Price Forecaster in the World
#1 Palladium Price Forecaster in the World
#1 Industrial Metals Price Forecaster in the World
#1 Copper Price Forecaster in the World
#1 Aluminum Price Forecaster in the World
#1 Nickel Price Forecaster in the World
#1 Tin Price Forecaster in the World
#1 Zinc Price Forecaster in the World
#2 Precious Metals Price Forecaster in the World
#2 Silver Price Forecaster in the World
#2 Lead Price Forecaster in the World
#2 Iron Ore Forecaster in the World

AGRICULTURAL PRICE TOP RANKINGS
#1 Coffee Price Forecaster in the World
#1 Cotton Price Forecaster in the World
#1 Sugar Price Forecaster in the World
#1 Soybean Price Forecaster in the World

FOREIGN EXCHANGE TOP RANKINGS

#1 Euro Forecaster in the World

#1 British Pound Forecaster in the World

#1 Swiss Franc Forecaster in the World

#1 Chinese RMB Forecaster in the World

#1 Russian Ruble Forecaster in the World

#1 Brazilian Real Forecaster in the World

#2 Turkish Lira Forecaster in the World

#3 Major Currency Forecaster in the World

#3 Canadian Dollar Forecaster in the World

#4 Japanese Yen Forecaster in the World

#5 Australian Dollar Forecaster in the World

#7 Mexican Peso Forecaster in the World

#1 EURCHF Forecaster in the World

#2 EURJPY Forecaster in the World

#2 EURGBP Forecaster in the World

#2 EURRUB Forecaster in the World

For more information about Prestige Economics:

www.prestigeeconomics.com

PUBLISHER

Prestige Professional Publishing, LLC was founded in 2011 to produce insightful and timely professional reference books. We are registered with the Library of Congress.

Published Titles

A Gentle Introduction to Audit and Due Diligence
Be the Shredder, Not the Shred
Commodity Prices 101
Electing Recession
Financial Risk Management Fundamentals
Futureproof Supply Chain
Jobs for Robots
Midterm Economics
Quantum: Computing Nouveau
Robot-Proof Yourself
Spikes: Growth Hacking Leadership
The Dumpster Fire Election
The Fog of Data
The Future of Energy
The Promise of Blockchain
The Robot and Automation Almanac — 2018
The Robot and Automation Almanac — 2019

Future Titles

Reading the Economic Tea Leaves
The Future of Finance is Now
The Future of Agriculture
The Future of Healthcare
The Robot and Automation Almanac — 2020

DISCLAIMER

FROM THE PUBLISHER

The following disclaimer applies to any content in this book:

This book is commentary intended for general information use only and is not investment advice. Prestige Professional Publishing, LLC does not make recommendations on any specific or general investments, investment types, asset classes, non-regulated markets, specific equities, bonds, or other investment vehicles. Prestige Professional Publishing, LLC does not guarantee the completeness or accuracy of analyses and statements in this book, nor does Prestige Professional Publishing, LLC assume any liability for any losses that may result from the reliance by any person or entity on this information. Opinions, forecasts, and information are subject to change without notice. This book does not represent a solicitation or offer of financial or advisory services or products; this book is only market commentary intended and written for general information use only. This book does not constitute investment advice. All links were correct and active at the time this book was published.

Prestige Professional Publishing, LLC

7101 Fig Vine Cove

Austin, Texas 78750

www.prestigeprofessionalpublishing.com

ISBN: 978-1-946197-31-3 *Paperback*

978-1-946197-32-0 *Ebook*